The
WISDOM
of
BUDDHISM

The
WISDOM
of
BUDDHISM

Compiled by Mel Thompson

ONEWORLD

OXFORD

THE WISDOM OF BUDDHISM
Oneworld Publications
(Sales and Editorial)
185 Banbury Road
Oxford OX2 7AR
England

http://www.oneworld-publications.com

Oneworld Publications
(US Marketing Office)
160 N. Washington St.
4th Floor, Boston
MA 02114
USA

© Mel Thompson 2000

ISBN 1–85168–226–0

Cover design by Design Deluxe, Bath
Typeset by Cyclops Media Productions
Printed and bound by Graphicom Srl, Vicenza, Italy

CONTENTS

PREFACE

THE TEACHING of the Buddha, and of those who have followed his path during the last two and a half millennia, is essentially concerned to promote two things: wisdom amd compassion.

The wisdom of Buddhism lies in its remorseless quest to see things as they really are, freed from the delusions created by greed, hatred and ignorance. It presents a world which is constantly changing and within which everything is interconnected. Also, it sees the idea of a permanent, fixed self, isolating itself from the world within which it is set, ever looking for satisfaction but frustrated by the impermanence of that at which it grasps, as a dangerous illusion and the source of suffering.

The natural response to such a vision of reality is a sense of oneness with all other living things. The letting go of the illusion of a separate, permanent and inherently existing self, leads to a self-understanding based on relationships, as a part of a greater, ever-changing whole. In Buddhist spirituality, this leads to a natural sense of compassion for all who suffer, sympathetic joy at the happiness of others, loving-kindness towards all living things, and equanimity in the face of life's changes and chances.

The Buddhist quest for reality is personal, and each individual is encouraged to follow the path in his or her own way. Hence, the extracts in this book are arranged according to the aspect of human experience to which they refer, beginning with the restless mind, whose dissatisfaction is the starting point of every quest for wisdom.

Other sections deal with training the mind to become aware of the present moment, to become calm through meditation, and to develop qualities that lead to a life of simplicity and holiness. The analysis of experience, and the ability to watch the workings of the mind, seeing which things lead to happiness and which to suffering, is essential to Buddhist training.

Through all this, however, is the fundamental conviction that the teachings of the Buddha simply point the way in which individuals can encounter the reality of life, and thereby overcome suffering. It is not a set of teachings to be accepted on trust, but an open invitation to explore one's own experience with radical honesty.

Of course, Buddhism developed in the East, and many earlier passages from Buddhist scriptures reflect Eastern thought and culture. By contrast, other passages in this book are taken from modern writers, whose intention it is to communicate the wisdom of Buddhism to Westerners. This is not to dilute the original teaching to make it more acceptable, but a recognition that every spiritual tradition changes as it encounters new situations. Buddhism is one such growing and changing reality, but it is hoped that the diversity of passages included here will reveal the underlying simplicity of the Buddha's teaching in a way that makes its wisdom relevant to all.

MEL THOMPSON

ENTERING THE DOOR

THE BUDDHA NATURE

HE BUDDHA-NATURE which is ours from the very beginning is like the sun which emerges from the clouds, or like a mirror which, when rubbed, regains its original purity and clarity.

> From Ho-shan's Memorial to the Tibetan King in
> *Buddhist Scriptures,* ed. CONZE

IT IS important to understand that buddha nature is not something we imagine or create from nothing. It is something that exists within each sentient being already, and the gradual method the Buddha taught is designed to awaken the ever-present buddha nature by instructing individuals at different levels of development exactly how to do this.

> *Awakening the Sleeping Buddha,* THE TWELFTH TAI SITUPA

LIFE IS boundless; it has an infinite horizon of positive development as well as an infinite danger of degeneration. There is an ultimate goal for human evolution, an enlightened state, a full development of wisdom, love, happiness, and power that is beyond even our wildest dreams, inconceivable to our habitual notions.

Materialists and nihilists have no room for such an ideal and so close off the possibility for themselves. Theistic mystics have identified such a life as the life of God and as possible for rarely blessed humans only through union with God. But Buddhists have identified such a state as that of an enlightened person, a perfect buddha. They consider it accessible to everyone, for anyone can and everyone will become enlightened buddhas themselves.

Inner Revolution, ROBERT THURMAN

EVEN THE gods long to be like the Buddhas who are awake and watch, who find peace in contemplation and who, calm and steady, find joy in renunciation.

It is a great event to be born a man; and his life is an ever-striving. It is not often he hears the doctrine of Truth; and a rare event is the arising of a Buddha.

Dhammapada, 181, 182

FACED WITH the difficulty of defining the Buddha mind, Buddhist teachers sometimes resort to analogy. Zen Buddhism refers to it as the circle whose centre is nowhere, and whose circumference is everywhere. The analogy of the mirror is also sometimes used. A mirror reflects whatever is placed in front of it, yet does not contain the images thus formed, still less *is it* these images. In the case of the Buddha mind, sense data and thoughts are analogous to the images, and the mind itself analogous to the mirror. Sense impressions and thoughts make their impressions upon the mind as images do in the mirror, but the mind is no more these impressions than the mirror is its reflections.

The aim of Buddhist practice is to prevent the Buddha mind from being obscured by the transitory images and impressions that pass constantly in and out of awareness. Only in this way can the Buddha mind be experienced in its 'unborn, unqualified' essence.

DAVID FONTANA, *The Authority of Experience*

EVERY SENTIENT being is ready to be enlightened at every moment. The only hindrance is not recognising the purity and limitlessness of buddha nature. We may have inklings

of our limitless quality, but we don't fully recognise it, so we become focused on the relative I, the self.

Awakening the Sleeping Buddha, THE TWELFTH TAI SITUPA

RIGHTLY SPEAKING, were it to be said of anyone: 'A being not subject to delusion has appeared in the world for the welfare and happiness of many, out of compassion for the world, for the good, welfare, and happiness of gods and humans', it is of me indeed that rightly speaking this should be said.

THE BUDDHA, *Mahasihanada Sutta, 63 (MN)*

THERE IS a simple way to become a buddha: When you refrain from unwholesome actions, are not attached to birth or death, and are compassionate toward all sentient beings, respectful to seniors and kind to juniors, not excluding or desiring anything, with no designing thoughts or worries, you will be called a buddha. Do not seek anything else.

Moon in a Dewdrop, ZEN MASTER DOGEN

THE RESTLESS MIND

I F WE can stop and be still, the mind will have a chance to be free, to contemplate its sufferings and let them go.

Looking Inward, K. KHAO-SUAN-LUANG

MUCH TALK, much worry,
and you're less than ever able to face things.
Be done with talk, be done with worry,
and there's no place you cannot pass through.

BHIKKHU MANGALO, *Entering the Stream*

T HE MIND is wavering and restless, difficult to guard and restrain: let the wise man straighten his mind as a maker of arrows makes his arrows straight.

The mind is fickle and flighty, it flies after fancies wherever it likes: it is difficult indeed to restrain. But it is a great good to control the mind; the mind self-controlled is a source of great joy.

Dhammapada, 33, 35

SINCE A shower of golden coins could not satisfy craving desires and the end of all pleasure is pain, how could a wise man find satisfaction even in the pleasures of the gods? When desires go, joy comes: the follower of Buddha finds this truth.

Men in their fear fly for refuge to mountains or forests, groves, sacred trees or shrines. But those are not a safe refuge, they are not the refuge that frees a man from sorrow.

He who goes for refuge to Buddha, to Truth and to those whom he taught, he goes indeed to a great refuge. Then he sees the four great truths: Sorrow, the cause of sorrow, the end of sorrow, and the path of eight stages which leads to the end of sorrow.

A man of true vision is not easy to find, a Buddha who is awake is not born everywhere. Happy are the people where such a man is born.

Happy is the birth of a Buddha, happy is the teaching of Dhamma, happy is the harmony of his followers, happy is the life of those who live in harmony.

Dhammapada, 186–94

LET US take a look at the mind of an ordinary worldly person. What we find is a grasshopper mind, a butterfly mind, chasing its fancies and impulses of the moment, the prey of stimuli and its own emotional reaction to them – a reaction that is largely a purely conditioned and blind one. A chain of linked associations, hopes, fears, memories, fantasies, regrets, stream constantly through the mind, triggered off by momentary contact with the outside world through the senses. It is a blind, never-ceasing, never-satisfied search for satisfaction, bewildered, aimless suffering. This is not reality, but a waking dream, a sequence of concepts and fantasies … the Buddha described such a mind as a restless monkey swinging from branch to branch in the quest for satisfying fruit through the endless jungle of conditioned events. The futility, unreality, and frustration inherent in such a mode of existence is startlingly self-apparent once one begins to see it clearly.

It is the purpose of Buddhism, and of religion in general, to reunite one with the Reality one has thus lost sight of due to one's ignorance in seeking the happiness for which one thirsts where it is not to be found – in the shadows and illusions of one's own mind.

BHIKKHU MANGALO, *Entering the Stream*

CONSCIOUSNESS IS an untamed horse,
The mind an unruly monkey.
If the spirit is overactive,
The body will sicken and die.

WANG MING

CHANGE AND GROWTH

IF EVERYTHING in existence were substantial and permanent, no one could grow old or learn anything; nothing could change, either for better or for worse; nothing could be improved, because there would be no room for it. This is common sense if you see emptiness simply. Emptiness provides the questions and the answers to all the questions, because it allows for movement and change. It allows for insight and realisation.

Awakening the Sleeping Buddha, THE TWELFTH TAI SITUPA

THE GLORY of the world is like a flower: it stands in full bloom in the morning and fades in the heat of the day.

Wherever you look, there is a rushing and a struggling, and an eager pursuit of pleasure. There is a panic flight from pain and death, and hot are the flames of burning desires. The world is vanity fair, full of changes and transformations. All is Samsara.

Is there nothing permanent in the world: is there in the universal turmoil no resting place where our troubled heart can find peace: is there nothing everlasting?

Oh, that we could have cessation of anxiety, that our burning desires would be extinguished! When shall the mind become tranquil and composed?

The Buddha, our Lord, was grieved at the ills of life. He saw the vanity of worldly happiness and sought salvation in the one thing that will not fade or perish, but will abide for ever and ever.

You who long for life, know that immortality is hidden in transiency. You who wish for happiness, without the sting of regret, lead a life of righteousness. You who yearn for riches, receive treasures that are eternal. Truth is wealth and a life of truth is happiness.

All compounds will be dissolved again, but the truths which determine all combinations and separations as laws of nature endure for ever and always. Bodies fall to dust, but the truths of the mind will not be destroyed.

The Teachings of Buddha, PAUL CARUS

THE BUDDHA said to a Novice: 'How long is the span of a man's life?'

'It is but a few days,' was the answer.

The Buddha said: 'You have not understood,' and asked another Novice, who replied: 'It is [like] the time taken to eat [a single meal].'

To this the Buddha replied in the same way and asked a third: 'How long is the span of a man's life?'

'It is like the time taken by a [single] breath,' was the reply.

'Excellent,' said the Buddha, 'You understand the Way.'

The Sutra of 42 Sections

IT IS helpful to reflect on impermanence. No matter how long our life is, there is a limit to it, is there not? When we think about the formation of the universe and of geological time, the lifetime of a human is very short...Under these circumstances, it is senseless to concentrate all your energy, mental as well as physical, on accumulating money and property. Since it is very clear that wealth is helpful only for this life, it is appropriate to reduce extreme greed.

The Meaning of Life from a Buddhist Perspective,
THE DALAI LAMA

WHEN WE look into our minds and observe it, we begin to see that everything is impermanent, rising and falling, coming and going. Nothing is really static. Yet what are we always trying to do? To make everything stay put! We are trying to hold on, to feel safe and secure. The natural order of things is to flow like a river, but the flow is so fast, changing so quickly, that is feels unstable. There is nothing to hold on to, nothing we can depend on; it is moving too quickly. There is only one time when we will be safe and secure: in a pine box! Only then will you be secure; only there on your nice, soft bed, on your comfortable pillow. You will look good in there, too! You will be very, very secure when you are dead, but then it will be too late to enjoy life.

Don't you know life is insecure, life is a risk? The moment you were born, the risk of your death arose at the same time. That is why we say that life and death cannot be two things; you can never separate them. How can you have only life with never any death? With life comes the guarantee of death. The moment a child is born, death is inevitable.

The Eye Never Sleeps, DENNIS GENPO MERZEL

THE PATH TO HAPPINESS

JUST LIKE a blind man
Discovering a jewel in a heap of rubbish,
Likewise by some coincidence
An Awakening Mind has been born in me.

A Guide to the Bodhisattva's Way of Life, SHANTIDEVA

WHAT WE are today comes from our thoughts of yesterday, and our present thoughts build our life to tomorrow: our life is the creation of our mind.

If a man speaks or acts with an impure mind, suffering follows him as the wheel of the cart follows the beast that draws the cart.

… If a man speaks or acts with a pure mind, joy follows him as his own shadow.

Dhammapada, 1, 2

I F WE examine our lives we will probably discover that most of our time and energy is directed towards mundane aims such as seeking material and emotional security, enjoying the pleasures of the senses, or achieving a good reputation. Although these things can make us happy for a short time, they are not able to provide the deep and lasting contentment we long for. Sooner or later our happiness turns into dissatisfaction and we find ourselves engaged in the pursuit of more worldly pleasures. Directly or indirectly, worldly pleasures cause us mental and physical suffering by stimulating attachment, jealousy, and frustration. Moreover, seeking to fulfil our own desires often brings us into conflict with others. If true fulfilment cannot be found in worldly pleasures, where can it be found? Happiness is a state of mind, therefore the real source of happiness lies in the mind, not in external conditions. If our mind is pure and peaceful we will be happy regardless of our external circumstances, but if it is impure and unpeaceful we will never find happiness, no matter how much we try to change our external conditions. The purpose of Dharma practice is to cultivate those states of mind that are conducive to peace and well-being, and to eradicate those that are not. Only human beings can do this. Animals can enjoy food and sex, find homes, hoard wealth, subdue their enemies, and protect their family, but they cannot completely eliminate suffering and achieve lasting happiness. It would be a great shame if we were to use our precious human life only to achieve results that even animals can achieve. If we wish to avoid such a wasted life and fulfil our real purpose of being born human we must devote ourselves to the practice of the States of the Path.

A Meditation Handbook, GESHE KELSANG GYATSO

THOSE WHO in their youth did not live in self-harmony, and who did not gain the true treasures of life, are later like long-legged old herons standing sad by a lake without fish.

Dhammapada, 155

CONFESS ALL your sins;
meditate joy all day and night.
Look to your body for what you have done before;
what will happen later depends on your mind.
When you have meditated this way for a long time,
the signs will arise progressively,
and you will obtain Buddhahood
in this very life.

Buddha's Lions, ABHAYADATTA

HAVING FIRMLY seized the Awakening Mind in this way,
A Conqueror's son must never waiver;
Always should he exert himself
To never stray from his practice.

In the case of reckless actions
Or of deeds not well considered,
Although a promise may have been made
It is fit to reconsider whether I should do them or not.

But how can I ever withdraw
From what has been examined by the great wisdom
Of the Buddhas and their Sons,
And even by many times by me myself?

If having made such a promise
I do not put it into action,
Then by deceiving every living being
What kind of rebirth shall I take?

A Guide to the Bodhisattva's Way of Life, SHANTIDEVA

A MAN becomes a herb-eater, a millet-eater, a raw-rice-eater, a wild-rice-eater, an eater of water-plants, of rice-husk-powder, of rice-scum, of the flowers of oil-seeds, grass or cow-dung, of forest roots and fruits, eating windfalls. He wears coarse hemp or mixed material, shrouds from corpses, rags, skins, grass, bark, shavings, blankets of human hair or horse-hair, the wings of owls. He is a plucker-out of hair and beard, devoted to this practice; he is a covered-thorn man, making his bed on them, sleeping alone in a garment of wet mud, living in the open air, accepting whatever seat is offered, living on filth and addicted to the practice, one who drinks no water and is addicted to the practice, or he dwells intent on the practice of going to bathe three times before evening.

A practiser of self-mortification may do all these things, but if his morality, his heart and his wisdom are not developed and brought to realisation, then indeed he is still far from being an ascetic or a Brahmin. But … when a monk develops non-enmity, non-ill-will and a heart full of loving-kindness and, abandoning the corruptions, realises and dwells in the uncorrupted deliverance of mind, the deliverance through wisdom, having realised it in this very life by his own insight, then … that monk is termed an ascetic and a Brahmin.

Mahasihanada Sutta, 15 (DN)

WHAT IS BUDDHISM?

ECAUSE OF Buddhism's emphasis on self-creation, there is no creator-deity, and thus from this viewpoint some people consider it, strictly speaking, not to be a religion. A Western Buddhist scholar told me, 'Buddhism is not a religion; it is a kind of science of mind.' In this sense, Buddhism does not belong to the category of religion. I consider this to be unfortunate, but in any case it means that Buddhism becomes closer to science. Furthermore, from the pure scientist's viewpoint, Buddhism naturally is considered a type of spiritual path. Again, it is unfortunate that we do not belong to the category of science. Buddhism thereby belongs to neither religion nor pure science, but this situation provides us with an opportunity to make a link, or a bridge, between faith and science.

The Meaning of Life from a Buddhist Perspective,
THE DALAI LAMA

THE QUESTION has often been asked: Is Buddhism a religion or a philosophy? It does not matter what you call it. Buddhism remains what it is whatever label you put on it. The label is immaterial …

In the same way Truth needs no label: it is neither Buddhist, Christian, Hindu or Moslem. It is not the monopoly of anybody. Sectarian labels are a hindrance to the independent understanding of Truth, and they produce harmful prejudices in men's minds.

What the Buddha Taught, WALPOLA RAHULA

BUDDHISM IS an education, not a religion. We do not worship the Buddha, we respect him as a teacher. His teachings enable us to leave suffering and attain happiness.

What does Buddha mean? 'Buddha' means enlightenment/ understanding. Complete understanding is when one realises the truth about life and the universe. It is when one is apart from all delusions.

The Teachings of the Ven Master CHIN KUNG in *What is Buddhism?*

SPIRITUALITY I take to be concerned with those qualities of the human spirit – such as love and compassion, a sense of responsibility, a sense of harmony – which bring happiness to both self and others. Whilst ritual and prayer, along with the questions of nirvana and salvation, are directly connected with religious faith, these inner qualities need not be, however. Thus there is no reason why the individual should not develop them, even to a high degree, without recourse to any religious or metaphysical belief system. This is why I sometimes say that religion is something we can perhaps do without. What we cannot do without are these basic spiritual qualities.

Ancient Wisdom, Modern World, THE DALAI LAMA

RADIATING LOVE

LOVE AND FRIENDSHIP

'HE INSULTED me, he hurt me, he defeated me, he robbed me.' Those who think such thoughts will not be free from hate.

'He insulted me, he hurt me, he defeated me, he robbed me.' Those who think not such thoughts will be free from hate.

For hate is not conquered by hate: hate is conquered by love. This is the law eternal.

Dhammapada, 3–5

GIFTS ARE great, the founding of viharas is meritorious, meditations and religious exercises pacify the heart, comprehension of the truth leads to Nirvana, but greater than all is loving kindness. As the light of the moon is sixteen times stronger than the light of all the stars, so loving kindness is sixteen times more efficacious in liberating the heart than all other religious accomplishments taken together.

Metta Sutta (trans. CARUS)

MENTALLY I create a happy and healthy aura of loving-kindness around me. By means of this aura I cut off all negative thoughts, all hostile vibrations. I am not affected by the evil thoughts of others.

I am fortified by my own thoughts of loving-kindness.

I radiate these loving thoughts of boundless goodwill towards all beings – above, below and around.

May I be able to identify myself with all without any distinction.

May all beings be well and happy! May all be free from suffering, troubles and worries! May they be free from anger, jealousy, envy and malice!

May all live in peace and harmony!

A meditation on loving-kindness, from *A Buddhist's Manual*

MAY CREATURES all abound
in weal and peace; may all
be blessed with peace always;
all creatures weak or strong,
all creatures great and small;

creatures unseen or seen,
dwelling afar or near,
born or awaiting birth,
– may all be blessed with peace!

Let none cajole or flout
his fellow anywhere;
let none wish others harm
in dudgeon or in hate.

Just as with her own life
a mother shields from hurt
her own, her only, child, –
let all-embracing thoughts
for all that lives be thine,

– an all-embracing love
for all the universe

in all its heights and depths
and breadth, unstinted love,
unmarred by hate within,
not rousing enmity.

So, as you stand or walk,
or sit, or lie, reflect
with all your might on this;
–'tis deemed 'a state divine'.

From the Sutta Nipata (trans. BURTT)

WHATEVER JOY there is in this world
All comes from desiring others to be happy,
And whatever suffering there is in this world
All comes from desiring myself to be happy.

But what need is there to say much more?
The childish work for their own benefit,
The Buddhas work for the benefit of others.
Just look at the difference between them!

A Guide to the Bodhisattva's Way of Life, SHANTIDEVA

MAY ALL animals be free from the fear
Of being eaten by one another;
May the hungry ghosts be as happy
As the men of the Northern Continent.

May they be satisfied
By a stream of milk pouring from the hand
Of the Noble Lord Avalokiteshvara,
And by bathing in it may they always be cooled.

May the blind see forms,
May the deaf hear sounds,
And just as it was with Mayadevi,
May pregnant women give birth without any pain.

May the naked find clothing,
The hungry find food;
May the thirsty find water
And delicious drinks.

May the poor find wealth,
Those weak with sorrow find joy;
May the forlorn find new hope,
Constant happiness and prosperity.

May all who are sick and ill
Quickly be freed from their illness,
And may every disease in the world
Never occur again.

May the frightened cease to be afraid
And those bound be freed;
May the powerless find power,
And may people think of benefiting one another.

A Guide to the Bodhisattva's Way of Life, SHANTIDEVA

COMPASSION AND love are not mere luxuries. As the source both of inner and external peace, they are fundamental to the continued survival of our species. On the one hand, they constitute non-violence in action. On the other, they are the source of all spiritual qualities of forgiveness, tolerance and all the virtues. Moreover they are the very thing that gives meaning to our activities and makes them constructive. There is nothing amazing about being highly educated; there is nothing amazing about being rich. Only if the individual has a warm heart do these attributes become worthwhile.

Ancient Wisdom, Modern World, THE DALAI LAMA

S IT UPON your meditation seat in a comfortable posture and visualise your mother of this life sitting before you. Contemplate how she carried you in her womb for almost ten months, and how during this time she experienced much suffering and inconvenience for you ... and, when you finally emerged from her womb, looking like a naked and helpless worm covered with blood and mucus, she took you lovingly in her arms and placed you to her soft flesh to give you warmth, gave you milk from her own breast, prepared food for you, cleaned the mucus from your nose and the excrement from your body, looked with a smiling countenance upon you, and at night sacrificed her own comfort and sleep for you ...

Meditate in this way until you appreciate her more than anything else, until your heart opens to her with love and the mere thought of her brings joy to your mind.

Exchanging Self for Other, GENDUN GYATSO

COMPASSION

IN BUDDHISM, love is based on wisdom. This is called compassion.

The Teachings of Ven Master CHIN KUNG
in What is Buddhism?

COMPASSION IS to understand the other person's subjective world without stealing anything. Stealing means taking over.

Zen Therapy, DAVID BRAZIER

UPON ALL I ever look
Everywhere impartially,
Without distinction of persons,
Or mind of love or hate,
I have no predilections
Nor any limitations;
Ever to all beings
I preach the Law equally;
As I preach to one person,
So I preach to all.

Ever I proclaim the Law,
Engaged in naught else;
Going, coming, sitting, standing,
Never am I weary of
Pouring it copiously on the world,
Like the all-enriching rain.
On honoured and humble, high and low,
Those of perfect character,
And those of imperfect,
Orthodox and heterodox,
Quick-witted and dull-witted,
Equally I rain the Law-rain
Unwearyingly.

From the Lotus Sutra (trans. BURTT)

WITH FOLDED hands I beseech
The Buddhas in all directions
To shine the lamp of the Dharma
For all bewildered in misery's gloom.

With folded hands I beseech
The Conquerors who wish to pass away,
To please remain for countless aeons

And not to leave the world in darkness.

Thus by the virtue collected
Through all that I have done,
May the pain of every living creature
Be completely cleared away.

May I be the doctor and the medicine
And may I be the nurse
For all sick beings in the world
Until everyone is healed.

May a rain of food and drink descend
To clear away the pain of thirst and hunger
And during the aeon of famine
May I myself change into food and drink.

May I become an inexhaustible treasure
For those who are poor and destitute;
May I turn into all things they could need
And may these be placed close beside them.

Without any sense of loss
I shall give up my body and enjoyments

As well as all my virtues of the three times
For the same of benefiting all.

A Guide to the Bodhisattva's Way of Life, SHANTIDEVA

COMPASSION ... ARISES from a clear understanding of karma. The principle of karma implies and confirms a deep interrelationship between all beings and all things. This interrelatedness among all things means that what touches one, touches all. This is the truth that all Buddhas and Bodhisattvas awaken to. The dichotomies we make between self and others, body and mind, and man and nature, are all fabrications and false. We thus, in a very real way, 'do unto ourselves what we do unto others', suggesting yet a deeper dimension of meaning to the long-standing Golden Rule.

Based on the teachings of Venerable Tripitaka Master
HSUAN HUA

ALL ACTIVITIES that benefit others are acts that reinforce the mind.

The Power of Buddhism, THE DALAI LAMA

THEN, WITH his heart filled with loving-kindness, he dwells suffusing one quarter, the second, the third, the fourth. Thus he dwells suffusing the whole world, upwards, downwards, across, everywhere, always with a heart filled with loving-kindness, abundant, unbounded, without hate or ill-will.

Just as a mighty trumpeter were with little difficulty to make a proclamation to the four quarters, so by this meditation ... by this liberation of the heart through loving-kindness he leaves nothing untouched, nothing unaffected in the sensuous sphere. This ... is the way to union with Brahma.

Tevijji Sutta, 76, 77 (DN)

MAY I be a protector for those without one,
A guide for all travellers on the way;
May I be a bridge, a boat and a ship
For all who wish to cross (the water)

May I be an island for those who seek one
And a lamp for those desiring light,
May I be a bed for all who wish to rest
And a slave for all who want a slave.

May I be a wishing jewel, a magic vase,
Powerful mantras and great medicine,
May I become a wish-fulfilling tree
And a cow of plenty for the world.

Just like space
And the great elements such as earth,
May I always support the life
Of all the boundless creatures.

And until they pass away from pain
May I also be a source of life
For all the realms of varied beings
That reach unto the ends of space.

A Guide to the Bodhisattva's Way of Life, SHANTIDEVA

DEALING WITH OTHER PEOPLE

MANY DO not know that we are here in this world to live in harmony. Those who know this do not fight against each other.

Dhammapada, 6

SPIRITUAL MATURITY in Buddhism is measured by one's capacity to acknowledge one's dependency on others.

The Ethics of Enlightenment, RONALD Y. NAKASONE

DO NOT be concerned with the faults of other persons. Do not see others' faults with a hateful mind. There is an old saying that if you stop seeing others' faults, then naturally seniors are venerated and juniors are revered. Do not imitate others' faults; just cultivate virtue. Buddha prohibited unwholesome actions, but did not tell us to hate those who practise unwholesome actions.

Moon in a Dewdrop, ZEN MASTER DOGEN

WHICHEVER OF us returns first from the village with almsfood prepares the seats, sets out the water for drinking and for washing, and puts the refuse bucket in its place. Whichever of us returns last eats any food left over, if he wishes; otherwise he throws it away where there is no greenery or drops it into water where there is no life. He puts away the seats and the water for drinking and for washing. He puts away the refuse bucket after washing it, and he sweeps out the refectory. Whoever notices that the pots of water for drinking, washing, or the latrine are low or empty takes care of them. If they are too heavy for him, he calls someone else by a signal of the hand and they move it by joining hands, but because of this we do not break out into speech. But every five days we sit together all night discussing the Dhamma (teaching). That is how we abide diligent, ardent, and resolute.

Upakkilesa Sutta, 14 (MN)

NOW, WHILE there is freedom to act,
I should always present a smiling face
And cease to frown and look angry:
I should be a friend and counsel of the world.

A Guide to the Bodhisattva's Way of Life SHANTIDEVA

I AM ... a Tibetan before I am Dalai Lama and I am human before I am Tibetan. So whilst as Dalai Lama I have a special responsibility to Tibetans, and as a monk I have special responsibility towards furthering inter-religious harmony, as a human being I have a much larger responsibility in respect of the whole human family – which indeed we all have. And since the majority does not practice religion, I am concerned with finding a way to serve all humanity without recourse to religious faith.

Ancient Wisdom, Modern World, THE DALAI LAMA

I SHOULD discreetly talk about the good qualities (of
    others)
And repeat those (that others) recount.
If my own good qualities are spoken about
I should just know and be aware that I have them.

All deeds (of others) are a source of a joy
That would be rare even if it could be bought with
    money.
Therefore I should be happy in finding this joy
In the good things that are done by others.

A Guide to the Bodhisattva's Way of Life, SHANTIDEVA

AFTER BANKEI had passed away, a blind man who lived near the master's temple told a friend: 'Since I am blind, I cannot watch a person's face, so I must judge his character by the sound of his voice. Ordinarily when I hear someone congratulate another upon his happiness or success, I also hear a secret tone of envy. When condolence is expressed for the misfortune of another, I hear pleasure and satisfaction, as if the one condoling was really glad there was something left to gain in his own world.

'In all my experience, however, Bankei's voice was always sincere. Whenever he expressed happiness, I heard nothing but happiness, and whenever he expressed sorrow, sorrow was all I heard.'

Zen Stories, 27

THOUGHTFUL LIVING

MORALITY AND THE PRECEPTS

H E WHO destroys life, who utters lies, who takes what is not given to him, who goes to the wife of another, who gets drunk with strong drinks – he digs up the very roots of his life.

Dhammapada, 346

I UNDERTAKE the rule of training to abstain from taking life.

I undertake the rule of training to abstain from taking the not given.

I undertake the rule of training to abstain from misuse of the senses.

I undertake the rule of training to abstain from wrong speech.

I undertake the rule of training to abstain from taking drugs and drinks which tend to cloud the mind.

The Five Precepts

DO NOT what is evil. Do what is good. Keep your mind pure. This is the teaching of Buddha.

Dhammapada, 183

HOLD NOT a sin of little worth, thinking 'this is little to me'. The falling of drops of water will in time fill a water-jar. Even so the foolish man becomes full of evil, although he gather it little by little.

… Let a man avoid the dangers of evil even as a merchant carrying much wealth, but with a small escort, avoids the dangers of the road, or as a man who loves his life avoids the drinking of poison.

As a man who has no wound on his hand cannot be hurt by the poison he may carry in his hand, since poison hurts not where there is no wound, the man who has no evil cannot be hurt by evil.

Dhammapada, 121, 123, 124

WATER DRIPPING ceaselessly
Will fill the four seas.
Specks of dust not wiped away
Will become the five mountains.

WANG MING

ABANDONING FALSE speech, the ascetic Gotama dwells refraining from false speech, a truth-speaker, one to be relied on, trustworthy, dependable, not a deceiver of the world. Abandoning malicious speech, he does not repeat there what he has heard here to the detriment of these, or repeat here what he has heard there to the detriment of those. Thus he is a reconciler of those at variance and an encourager of those at one, rejoicing in peace, loving it, delighting in it, one who speaks up for peace. Abandoning harsh speech, he refrains from it. He speaks whatever is blameless, pleasing to the ear, agreeable, reaching the heart, urbane, pleasing and attractive to the multitude. Abandoning idle chatter, he speaks at the right time, what is correct and to the point, of Dhamma and discipline. He is a speaker whose words are to be treasured, seasonable, reasoned, well-defined and connected with the goal.

Brahmajala Sutta, 1, 9 (DN)

AND WHAT, friends is the unwholesome? ... Killing living beings is unwholesome; taking what is not given is unwholesome; misconduct in sensual pleasures is unwholesome; false speech is unwholesome; malicious speech is unwholesome; harsh speech is unwholesome; gossip is unwholesome; covetousness is unwholesome; ill will is unwholesome; wrong view is unwholesome. This is called the unwholesome. And what is the root of the unwholesome? Greed is a root of the unwholesome; hate is a root of the unwholesome; delusion is a root of the unwholesome.

Sammaditthi Sutta, 4, 5 (MN)

ALTHOUGH ENEMIES such as hatred and craving
Have neither any arms nor legs,
And are neither courageous nor wise,
How have I been used like a slave by them?

For while they dwell within my mind
At their pleasure they cause me harm,
Yet I patiently endure them without any anger;
But this is an inappropriate and shameful time for
patience.

A Guide to the Bodhisattva's Way of Life, SHANTIDEVA

MANY GODS and men, wishing for well-being, have pondered over those things that constitute auspicious performances. Tell us what is the highest auspicious performance (great happiness or blessing).

Not to associate with fools, but to associate with the wise and to honour those who are worthy of honour ...

To reside in a congenial environment, to have done meritorious deeds in the past and to set oneself in the right course ...

A good all-round education, (appreciation of) the Arts, a highly trained discipline and pleasant speech ...
Supporting one's father and mother, cherishing wife and children and a peaceful occupation ...

Liberality, righteous conduct, the helping of relatives and blameless actions ...

Ceasing and abstaining from evil, abstention from intoxicating drinks and diligence in virtue ...

Reverence, humility, contentment, gratitude and timely hearing of the Dhamma ...

Morality and the Precepts ❧ 63

Forbearance, obedience, concourse with exemplars of the
Dhamma-life and taking part in religious discussions ...

Self control, chastity, perception of the Noble Truths and the
realisation of Nibbana ...

If one's mind is sorrowless, stainless and secure (in Nibbana) and
is not disturbed when touched by worldly vicissitudes ...

Those who, thus acting, are everywhere unconquered, attain
happiness everywhere – to them these are the most
auspicious performances.

Mangala Sutta

THE PURSUIT of the enjoyment of one whose pleasure is linked
to sensual desires – low, vulgar, coarse, ignoble, and
unbeneficial – is a state beset by suffering, vexation,
despair and fever, and it is the wrong way.

Aranavibhanga Sutta, 4 (MN)

SKILFUL ACTION

TANZAN AND Ekido were once travelling together down a muddy road. A heavy rain was still falling.

Coming around a bend, they met a lovely girl in a silk kimono and sash, unable to cross the intersection.

'Come on, girl,' said Tanzan at once, and lifting her in his arms, he carried her over the mud.

Ekido did not speak again until that night when they reached a lodging temple. Then he no longer could restrain himself.

'We monks don't go near females,' he told Tanzan, 'especially not young and lovely ones. It is dangerous. Why did you do that?'

'I left the girl there,' said Tanzan. 'Are you still carrying her?'

Zen Stories, 14

WHENEVER I have distracted thoughts, the wish to
verbally belittle others,
Feelings of self-importance or self-satisfaction;
When I have the intention to describe the faults of
others,
Pretensions and the thought to deceive others;

Whenever I am eager for praise
Or have the desire to blame others;
Whenever I have the wish to speak harshly and cause
dispute;
At (all) such times I should remain like a piece of
wood.

Whenever I desire material gain, honour or fame;
Whenever I seek attendants or a circle of friends,
And when in my mind I wish to be served;
At (all) these times I should remain like a piece of
wood.
Whenever I have the wish to decrease or to stop
working for others
And the desire to pursue my welfare alone,
If (motivated by such thoughts), a wish to say
something occurs,

At these times I should remain like a piece of wood.

Whenever I have impatience, laziness, cowardice,
Shamelessness or the desire to talk nonsense;
If thoughts of partiality arise,
At these times too I should remain like a piece of
wood.

A Guide to the Bodhisattva's Way of Life, SHANTIDEVA

WHICH ARE the six ways of wasting one's substance … ?
Addiction to strong drink and sloth-producing drugs is
one way of wasting one's substance, haunting the
streets at unfitting times is one, attending fairs is one, being
addicted to gambling is one, keeping bad company is one,
habitual idleness is one.

There are these six dangers attached to addiction to
strong drink and sloth-producing drugs: present waste of
money, increased quarrelling, liability to sickness, loss of good
name, indecent exposure of one's person, and weakening of the
intellect.

There are these six dangers attached to haunting the
streets at unfitting times: one is defenceless and without
protection, and so are one's wife and children, and so is one's

property; one is suspected of crimes, and false reports are pinned on one, and one encounters all sorts of unpleasantness.

There are these six dangers attached to frequenting fairs: [One is always thinking:] 'Where is there dancing? Where is there singing? Where are they playing music? Where are they reciting? Where is there hand-clapping? Where are the drums?'

There are these six dangers attached to gambling: the winner makes enemies, the loser bewails his loss, one waste's one's present wealth, one's word is not trusted in the assembly, one is despised by one's friends and companions, one is not in demand for marriage, because a gambler cannot afford to maintain a wife.

There are these six dangers attached to keeping bad company: any gambler, any glutton, any drunkard, any cheat, any trickster, any bully is his friend, his companion.

There are these six dangers attached to idleness: Thinking 'It's too cold', one does not work; thinking 'It's too hot', one does not work; thinking 'It's too early', one does not work; thinking 'It's too late', one does not work; thinking 'I'm too hungry', one does not work; thinking 'I'm too full', one does not work.

Sigalaka Sutta, 7–13 (DN)

I SHOULD desist from inconsiderately and noisily
Moving around chairs and so forth,
As well as from violently opening doors:
I should always delight in humility.

The stork, the cat and the thief,
By moving silently and carefully,
Accomplish what they desire to do;
A Bodhisattva too should always behave in this way.

A Guide to the Bodhisattva's Way of Life, SHANTIDEVA

THERE ARE two types of heroes in this world: those who do not commit transgressions and those who, having done so, are capable of repentance.

From the letters of Patriarch YIN KUANG

THE COMMON disease of sentient beings is to be diligent and earnest when catastrophe strikes but lax and remiss in normal times.

MASTER YIN KUANG, *letter 22*

WHEN TALKING I should speak from my heart and on
what is relevant.
Making the meaning clear and the speech pleasing,
I should not speak out of desire or hatred
But in gentle tones and in moderation.

A Guide to the Bodhisattva's Way of Life, SHANTIDEVA

THE PERFECTIONS such as generosity
Are progressively more exalted
But for a little (morality) I should not forsake a great
(gift).
Principally I should consider what will be of the most
benefit to others.

When this is understood,
I should strive for the welfare of others.
The Far-Seeing Merciful Ones have allowed (a
Bodhisattva)
To do some actions that (for others) were forbidden.

A Guide to the Bodhisattva's Way of Life, SHANTIDEVA

AS A child I am unable to increase my wealth,
And as a youth what can I do (being unable to afford a
    wife)?
At the end of my life when I have the wealth,
Being an old man, what good will sex be then?

Some evil and lustful people
Wear themselves out by working all day
And when they return home (in the evening)
Their exhausted bodies lie prostrate like corpses.

Some have the suffering of being disturbed with travel
And having to go a long way from home.
Although they long for their spouses,
They do not see them for years at a time.

And some who wish for benefit
Due to confusion, even sell themselves for the sake of
    (women and the like):
But not attaining what they wish,
They are aimlessly driven by the winds of others'
    actions.

A Guide to the Bodhisattva's Way of Life, SHANTIDEVA

EVERY ACTION we perform leaves an imprint on our very subtle mind, and each imprint eventually gives rise to its own effect. Our mind is like a field and performing actions is like sowing seeds in that field. Virtuous actions sow seeds of future happiness and non-virtuous actions sow seeds of future suffering.

A Meditation Handbook, GESHE KELSANG GYATSO

JUST AS medicine and poison
can be identical in themselves
and yet give rise to two different effects,
so one is avoided and the other is readily taken,
although they have one nature;
there is no difference.
The masters who realise this do not renounce things.
Those who are not masters must do so,
for lacking realisation, they wander in samsara.

Buddha's Lions, ABHAYADATTA

IN BUDDHISM ... the most important considerations are the results of our actions; we have to distinguish what to do and what not to do in terms of determining what can be accomplished. With such a background, activities that are completely prohibited in the scriptures on discipline are not only allowed but are required under certain circumstances – they *must* be done if they will be beneficial. Just as, in medical treatment, different medicines are used even by the same person under new circumstances, so when furthering the process of purifying the mind, different circumstances or stages call for the implementation of different techniques.

The Meaning of Life from a Buddhist Perspective,
THE DALAI LAMA

THE ENVIRONMENT

I F THE minds of the people are impure, their land is also impure, but if their minds are pure, so is their land. There are not two lands, pure and impure in themselves. The difference lies solely in the good or evil of our minds.

On Attaining Buddhahood, NICHIREN DAISHONIN

A LL BEINGS tremble before danger, all fear death. When a man considers this, he does not kill or cause to kill.
All beings fear before danger, life is dear to all. When a man considers this, he does not kill or cause to kill.

He who for the sake of happiness hurts others who also want happiness, shall not hereafter find happiness.

He who for the sake of happiness does not hurt others who also want happiness, shall hereafter find happiness.

Dhammapada, 129–132

A s THE bee takes the essence of a flower and flies away without destroying its beauty and perfume, so let the sage wander in this life.

Dhammapada, 49

W ESTERN SOCIETIES have for centuries taken it as read that humanity's greatest challenge is the conquest and subjection of nature. The traditional oriental view could hardly be more different: it is that humanity is a *part* of nature, not a being in rivalry with it. It is possible that the difference between the two views is a result of the disparity between the oriental and occidental views of life itself ...

Life can be understood only from a vantage point which integrates all of its activities as well as disciplines such as physics and chemistry. What we need today is a philosophy and religion that can foster exactly this sort of holistic view – a view that encompasses not just the individual but the Cosmos as a whole.

Unlocking the Mysteries of Birth and Death, DAISAKU IKEDA

PRACTICAL LIVING

THE DHARMA of the Tathagata (Buddha) does not require a person to go into homelessness or to resign the world, unless that person feels called upon to do so; but the Dharma of the Tathagata requires everyone to free oneself from the illusion of self, to cleanse one's heart, to give up the thirst for pleasure and lead a life of righteousness.

And whatever individuals do, whether they remain in the world as artisans, merchants, and officers of the king, or retire from the world and devote themselves to a life of religious meditation, let them put their whole heart into their task; let them be diligent and energetic, and, if they are like the lotus, which, although it grows in the water, yet remains untouched by the water, if they struggle in life without cherishing envy or hatred, if they live in the world not a life of self but a life of truth, then surely joy, peace, and bliss will dwell in their minds.

The Teachings of Buddha, PAUL CARUS

THERE ARE four types who can be seen as loyal friends: the friend who is a helper is one, the friend who is the same in happy and unhappy times is one, the friend who points out what is good for you is one, and the friend who is sympathetic is one.

The helpful friend can be seen to be a loyal friend in four ways: he looks after you when you are inattentive, he looks after your possessions when you are inattentive, he is a refuge when you are afraid, and when some business is to be done he lets you have twice what you ask for.

The friend who is the same in happy and unhappy times can be seen to be a loyal friend in four ways: he tells you his secrets, he guards your secrets, he does not let you down in misfortune, he would even sacrifice his life for you.

The friend who points out what is good for you can be seen to be a loyal friend in four ways: he keeps you from wrongdoing, he supports you in doing good, he informs you of what you did not know, and he points out the path to heaven.

The sympathetic friend can be seen to be a loyal friend in four ways: he does not rejoice at your misfortune, he rejoices in your good fortune, he stops others who speak against you, and he commends others who speak in praise of you.

Sigalaka Sutta, 21–5 (DN)

NEITHER NAKEDNESS, nor entangled hair, nor uncleanliness, nor fasting, nor sleeping on the ground, nor covering the body with ashes, nor ever-squatting, can purify a man who is not pure from doubts and desires.

But although a man may wear fine clothing, if he lives peacefully; and is good, self-possessed, has faith and is pure; and if he does not hurt any living being, he is a holy Brahmin, a hermit of seclusion, a monk called a Bhikkhu.

Dhammapada, 141, 142

OBEY THE nature of things
and you will walk freely and undisturbed.

Verses on the Faith Mind, CHIEN-CHIH SENG-TS'AN

BUDDHISM AIMS at creating a society where the ruinous struggle for power is renounced; where calm and peace prevail away from conquest and defeat; where the persecution of the innocent is vehemently denounced; where one who conquers oneself is more respected than those who conquer millions by military or economic warfare; where hatred is conquered by kindness, and evil by goodness; where enmity, jealousy, ill-will and greed do not infect men's minds; where compassion is the driving force of action; where all, including the least of living things, are treated with fairness, consideration and love; where life in peace and harmony, in a world of material contentment, is directed toward the highest and noblest aim, the realisation of the Ultimate Truth, Nirvana.

What the Buddha Taught, WALPOLA RAHULA

A SON should minister to his mother and father. 'Having been supported by them, I will support them. I will perform their duties for them. I will keep up the family tradition. I will be worthy of my heritage. After my parents' deaths I will distribute gifts on their behalf.'

Parents, so ministered to by their son … will reciprocate: they will restrain him from evil, support him in doing good, teach him some skill, find him a suitable wife and, in due time, hand over his inheritance to him.

There are five ways in which a husband should minister to his wife … : by honouring her, by not disparaging her, by not being unfaithful to her, by giving authority to her, by providing her with adornments. And a wife, thus ministered to by her husband … will reciprocate: by properly organising her work,

by being kind to the servants, by not being unfaithful, by protecting stores, and by being skilful and diligent in all she has to do.

A man should minister to his friends and companions: by gifts, by kindly words, by looking after their welfare, by treating them like himself, and by keeping his word. And friends and companions, thus ministered to by a man ... will reciprocate: by looking after him when he is inattentive, by looking after his property when he is inattentive, by being a refuge when he is afraid, and not deserting him when he is in trouble and by showing concern for his children.

A master should minister to his servants and workpeople ... by arranging their work according to their strengths, by supplying them with food and wages, by looking after them when they are ill, by sharing special delicacies with them, and by letting them off work at the right time. And servants and workpeople thus ministered to by their master ... will reciprocate: they will get up before him, go to bed after him, take only what they are given, do their work properly, and be bearers of his praise and good repute.

Sigalaka Sutta, 28, 30, 31, 32 (DN)

MODERATION

THOSE WHO fill their lamps with water will not dispel the darkness, and those who try to light a fire with rotten wood will fail. And how can anyone be free from self by leading a wretched life, if that person does not succeed in quenching the fire of lust, if that person still hankers after either worldly or heavenly pleasures. But those in whom self has become extinct are free from lust; they will desire neither worldly nor heavenly pleasures, and the satisfaction of their natural wants will not defile them. However, let them be moderate, let them eat and drink according to the needs of the body.

Sensuality is enervating; the self-indulgent are slaves to their passions, and pleasure-seeking is degrading and vulgar.

But to satisfy the necessities of life is not evil. To keep the body in good health is a duty, for otherwise we shall not be able to trim the lamp of wisdom, and keep our mind strong and clear. Water surrounds the lotus flower, but does not wet its petals.

The Teachings of Buddha, PAUL CARUS

ONE SHOULD not pursue sensual pleasure, which is low, vulgar, coarse, ignoble, and unbeneficial; and one should not pursue self-mortification, which is painful, ignoble, and unbeneficial. The Middle Way discovered by the Tathagata (the Buddha) avoids both extremes; giving vision, giving knowledge, it leads to peace, to direct knowledge, to enlightenment, to Nibbana.

Aranavibhanga Sutta, 3 (MN)

HOW CAN you obtain wealth by just wishful thinking?
Give up these daydreams,
    which are like the son of a barren woman.
The best body has the nature of the sky.
Contemplate that your mind is as bright as the many
    stars
        and you will become like the god of wealth
        himself.
When these things become evident,
    then everything you desire will arise.

Buddha's Lions, ABHAYADATTA

MOVING BEYOND SELF

THE NATURE OF THE SELF

HOLDING THIS body as 'mine',
Why, mind, do you guard it so?
Since you and it are separate,
What use can it be to you?

Why, confused mind,
Do you not hold only a clean, wooden form?
Just what is the point of guarding
This putrid, dirt-filled machine?

First of all, mentally separate
The layers of skin (from the flesh)
And then with the scalpel of discrimination
Separate the flesh from the skeletal frame.

And having split open even the bones
Look right down into the marrow,
While examining this ask yourself,
'Where is its essence?'

If, even when searching with such effort
You can apprehend no essence,

Then why with so much attachment
Are you still guarding this body now?

If servants are not given clothing and so forth
When they are unable to be employed,
Then why do you exhaust yourself looking after the
    flesh alone
When even though caring for the body, it goes
    elsewhere?

Now having paid my body its wages,
I shall engage it in making my life meaningful.
But if my body is of no benefit
Then I shall not give it anything.

I should conceive of my body as a boat,
A mere support for coming and going,
And in order to benefit all others
Transform it into a wish-fulfilling body.

A Guide to the Bodhisattva's Way of Life, SHANTIDEVA

B Y ATTENDING to things unfit for attention and by not attending to things fit for attention, both unarisen taints arise in him and arisen taints increase.

This is how he attends unwisely: 'Was I in the past? Was I not in the past? What was I in the past: How was I in the past? Having been what, what did I become in the past? Shall I be in the future: Shall I not be in the future? What shall I be in the future? How shall I be in the future?' or else he is inwardly perplexed about the present thus: 'Am I? Am I not? What am I? How am I? Where has this being come from? Where will it go?'

When he attends unwisely in this way, one of six views arises in him. The view 'self exists for me' arises in him as true and established; or the view 'no self exists for me' arises in him as true and established; or the view 'I perceive self with self' arises in him as true and established; or the view 'I perceive not-self with self' arises in him as true and established; or the view 'I perceive self with not-self' arises in him as true and established; or else he has some such view as this: 'It is this self of mine that speaks and feels and experiences here and there the result of good and bad actions; but this self of mine is permanent, everlasting, eternal, not subject to change, and it will endure as long as eternity.' This speculative view, Bhikkhus (monks), is called the thicket of views, the wilderness of views, the contortion of views, the vacillation of views, the fetter of views, Fettered by the fetter of views, the untaught ordinary person is not freed from birth, ageing, and death, from sorrow, lamentation, pain, grief, and despair; he is not freed from suffering, I say.

Sabbasava Sutta, 7, 8 (MN)

BOTH BODY and mind are things that belong to the I, and the I is the owner, but, aside from mind and body, there is no separate, independent entity of I. There is every indication that the I exists; yet, under investigation, you cannot find it. For example, the Dalai Lama's I must be within the confines of this area circumscribed by my body; there is no other place it could possibly be found. This is definite; it is for sure. However, if you investigate within this area what is the true Dalai Lama, the true Tenzin Gyatso, is, besides this body and mind the I does not have its own substance. Still, the Dalai Lama is a fact, a man, a monk, a Tibetan, someone who can speak, who can drink, who can sleep, who can enjoy; is it not so? This is sufficient to prove that something exists, even though it cannot be found.

The Meaning of Life from a Buddhist Perspective,
THE DALAI LAMA

UNLESS WE investigate ... we naturally have the view that we have a body that has its own independent existence. We feel that we can see and point to this self-existing body. However, whenever we see or point to our body we are seeing and pointing to *parts* of our body. We should investigate this point carefully. When we say we see our body, what do we in fact see? We see only the parts of our body – our arms, legs and so forth. When we look at our body there is nothing that we see that is not a part of our body and if something is a part of our body, it is necessarily not our body ...

Our body appears vividly to our mind and seems to exist from its own side. However ... if we investigate we are unable to find our body and we discover that it has no existence of its own, but is merely imputed by our mind ... As long as we believe that it has its own inherent existence, our body can be a source of fear and pain, but when we realise it is merely imputed by our mind, these fears and so forth will decrease and eventually disappear ...

Heart of Wisdom, GESHE KELSANG GYATSO

OUR CONSCIOUSNESS of 'self' forms the framework whereby we support our world-view. Our perceived division of the Universe into two parts – 'self' and 'other', or internal and external – arises from our consciousness of 'self'. This consciousness likewise gives rise to other dualities: for example, the duality of mind and body (in which we somehow regard the mind as being our true self whereas the body is not), the duality of the material and the spiritual, or the duality of mankind and nature. Dualistic thinking like this has underlain the evolution of modern civilisation, but it is also the root of many of modern civilisation's present crises.

Buddhism points the way to the resolution of such crises by demonstrating the truth that our lives are not limited to the self alone but encompass other people, the world and even the Universe. Perhaps nowhere do we find a better exposition of this idea, that the individual and the Cosmos are inseparable, than in the principle of *ichinen sanzen*, which has it that a single moment of life possesses three thousand realms.

Unlocking the Mysteries of Birth and Death, DAISAKU IKEDA

EVERY MOMENT the subatomic particles of which the body is composed arise and pass away. Every moment the mental functions appear and disappear, one after another. Everything inside oneself, physical and mental, just as the world outside, is changing every moment. Previously we may have known that this was true; we may have understood it intellectually. Now, however, by the practice of *vipashyana-bhavana* (insight meditation), we experience the reality of impermanence directly within the framework of the body. The direct experience of the transitory sensations proves to us our ephemeral nature.

S.N. GOENKA *in Entering the Stream*

'SISTERS, WHAT do you think? Is the eye ... the ear ... the nose ... the tongue ... the body ... the mind permanent or impermanent?'

'Impermanent, venerable sir.' ...

'Are forms ... sounds ... odours ... flavours ... tangibles ... mind-objects permanent or impermanent?'

'Impermanent, venerable sir.' ...

'Is what is impermanent, suffering, and subject to change fit to be regarded thus: "This is mine, this I am, this is my self?" '

'No, venerable sir ... We have already seen this well as it actually is with proper wisdom thus: "These six external bases are impermanent." ' ...

'Sisters, suppose an oil-lamp is burning: its oil is impermanent and subject to change, its wick is impermanent and subject to change, its flame is impermanent and subject to change, and its radiance is impermanent and subject to change. Now would anyone be speaking rightly who spoke thus: "While this oil-lamp is burning, its oil, wick, and flame are impermanent and subject to change, but its radiance is permanent, everlasting, eternal, not subject to change?" '

'No, venerable sir ... Because each feeling arises in dependence upon its corresponding condition, and with the cessation of its corresponding condition, the feeling ceases.'

Nandakovada Sutta, 7, 9, 10 (MN)

THE PHENOMENAL world is the result of thought. Therefore, when the mind is free from thought, it returns to its original nature, which is the ultimate reality. This is the same as the effect of the great cause for which all Buddhas appear in the world. Buddhas appear to help people attain enlightenment, which in Zen terms is to see their original face. Ordinary people cannot see their original face because of two extremes: they are attached to phenomena, and they are attached to self, both of which they mistakenly think of as real. If they awaken to the cosmic truth that both phenomena and self are illusory, they will realise prajna, the Buddha-knowledge that will lead them to enlightenment. They will be able to go beyond the phenomenal realm to arrive at ultimate reality.

The Complete Book of Zen, WONG KIEW KIT

FOLLOWING THE WAY

O NOT think about the shortcomings of others, but instead examine your own faults and expel them as if they were poison.

Do not think about your own qualities, but dwell on the virtuous qualities of others and venerate them as if you were their servant.

ATISHA

WILL NOT the ocean of joy
That shall exist when all beings are free
Be sufficient for me?
What am I doing wishing for my liberation alone?

Therefore, although working for the benefit of others,
I shall not be conceited or (count myself) wonderful.
And because of the joy there is in solely doing this,
I should have no hope for any ripening-effect.

A Guide to the Bodhisattva's Way of Life, SHANTIDEVA

EVEN AS on a heap of rubbish thrown away by the side of the road a lotus flower may grow and blossom with its pure perfume giving joy to the soul, in the same way among the blind multitudes shines pure the light of wisdom of the student who follows the Buddha, the one who is truly awake.

Dhammapada, 58, 59

ABANDONING WORLDLY desires, he dwells with a mind freed from worldly desires, and his mind is purified from them. Abandoning ill-will and hatred ... and by compassionate love for the welfare of all living beings, his mind is purified of ill-will and hatred. Abandoning sloth and torpor ... perceiving light, mindful and clearly aware, his mind is purified of sloth and torpor. Abandoning worry-and-flurry ... and with an inwardly calmed mind his heart is purified of worry-and-flurry. Abandoning doubt, he dwells with doubt left behind, without uncertainty as to what things are wholesome, his mind is purified of doubt.

Just as a man who had taken a loan to develop his business, and whose business had prospered, might pay off his old debts, and with what is left over could support a wife ...

Just as a man who was ill, suffering, terribly sick, with no appetite and weak in body, might after a time recover, and regain his appetite and bodily strength ...

Just as a man might be bound in prison, and after a time he might be freed from his bonds without any loss with no deduction from his possessions ...

Just as a man might be a slave, not his own master, dependent on another, unable to go where he liked, and after some time he might be freed from slavery ...

Just as a man, laden with goods and wealth, might go on a long journey through the desert where food was scarce and danger abounded, and after a time he would get through the desert and arrive safe ... he would rejoice and be glad about that.

As long, Sire, as a monk does not perceive the disappearance of the five hindrances in himself, he feels as if in debt, in sickness, in bonds, in slavery, on a desert journey. But when he perceives the disappearance of the five hindrances in himself, it is as if he were freed from debt, from sickness, from bonds, from slavery, from the perils of the desert.

And when he knows that these five hindrances have left him, gladness arises in him, from gladness comes delight, from the delight in his mind his body is tranquillised, with a tranquil body he feels joy, and with joy his mind is concentrated.

Samannaphala Sutta, 68–75 (DN)

IT IS a joy to see the noble and good, and to be with them makes one happy. If one were able never to see fools, then one could be for ever happy!

He who has to walk with fools has a long journey of sorrow, because to be with a fool is as painful as to be with an enemy; but the joy of being with the wise is like the joy of meeting a beloved kinsman.

If you find a man who is constant, awake to the inner light, learned, long-suffering, endowed with devotion, a nobleman – follow this good and great man even as the moon follows the path of the stars.

Dhammapada, 206–8

NEVER SHOULD I look around
Distractedly for no purpose:
With a resolute mind
I should always keep my eyes cast downwards.

But in order to relax the gaze
For a short while I should look around,
And if someone appears in my field of vision
I should look at him and say, 'Welcome.'

A Guide to the Bodhisattva's Way of Life, SHANTIDEVA

SUPPOSE A man in the course of a journey saw a great expanse of water, whose near shore was dangerous and fearful and whose further shore was safe and free from fear, but there was no ferryboat or bridge going to the far shore ... Then the man collected grass, twigs, branches and leaves and bound them together into a raft, and supported by the raft and making an effort with his hands and feet, he got safely across to the far shore. Then, having got safely across to the far shore he might think thus: 'This raft has been very helpful to me ... Suppose I were to hoist it on my head or load it on my shoulder, and then go wherever I want.' Now, Bhikkhus (monks), what do you think? By doing so, would that man be doing what should be done with that raft? (Or) he might think thus: 'This raft has been very helpful to me ... Suppose I were to haul it onto dry land or set it adrift in the water, and then go wherever I want.' Now Bhikkhus (monks), it is by doing so that that man would be doing what should be done with that raft. So I have shown you how the Dhamma (teaching) is similar to a raft, being for the purpose of crossing over, not for the purpose of grasping.

Alagaddupama Sutta, 13 (MN)

BUDDHIST PRACTICE is a process of transformation through purification that brings out the best of what is already there. It does not make people into what they are not, nor import any new material. It allows your ultimate identity as an enlightened being to emerge as you overcome the relative delusions and defilements that mask your buddha nature. It is transformation into your ultimate self.

Awakening the Sleeping Buddha, THE TWELFTH TAI SITUPA

> IF ONE can find a worthy friend,
> A virtuous, steadfast companion,
> Then overcome all threats of danger
> And walk with him content and mindful.
>
> But if one finds no worthy friend,
> No virtuous, steadfast companion,
> Then as a king leaves his conquered realm,
> Walk like a tusker in the woods alone.

Upakkilesa Sutta, 6 (MN)

WHEN PEOPLE start to meditate or to work with any kind of spiritual discipline, they often think that somehow they're going to improve, which is a sort of subtle aggression against who they really are. It's a bit like saying, 'If I jog, I'll be a much better person.' 'If I could only get a nicer house, I'd be a better person.' 'If I could meditate and calm down, I'd be a better person.' Or the scenario may be that they find fault with others; they might say, 'If it weren't for my husband, I'd have a perfect marriage.' 'If it weren't for the fact that my boss and I can't get on, my job would be just great.' And 'If it weren't for my mind, my meditation would be excellent.'

But loving-kindness – *maitri* – towards ourselves does not mean getting rid of anything. Maitri means that we can still be crazy after all these years. We can still be angry after all these years. We can still be timid or jealous or full of feelings of unworthiness. The point is not to try to change ourselves. Meditation practice isn't about trying to throw ourselves away and become something better. It's about befriending who we are already. The ground of practice is you or me or whoever we are right now, just as we are. That's the ground, that's what we study, that's what we come to know with tremendous curiosity and interest.

PEMA CHÖDRÖN, *Entering the Stream*

ATTITUDES AND MOTIVES

HAVING SEEN the mistakes in (cherishing) myself
And the ocean of good in (cherishing) others,
I shall completely reject all selfishness
And accustom myself to accepting others.

In the same way as the hands and so forth
Are regarded as limbs of the body,
Likewise why are embodied creatures
Not regarded as limbs of life?

Through acquaintance has the thought of 'I' arisen
Towards this impersonal body;
So in a similar way, why should it not arise
Towards other living beings?

When I work in this way for the sake of others,
I should not let conceit or (the feeling that I am)
    wonderful arise.
It is just like feeding myself –
I hope for nothing in return.

Therefore just as I protect myself
From unpleasant things however slight,
In the same way I should habituate myself
To have a compassionate and caring mind for others.

Thus whoever wishes to quickly afford protection
To both himself and other beings
Should practise that holy secret;
The exchanging of self for others.

A Guide to the Bodhisattva's Way of Life, SHANTIDEVA

WORRIES ARISE from the mind. You are wise if you do not let things worry you. Nothing and nobody can make you worry without your permission.

If we wish to bring peace to the world, we must start by changing our evil ways. World peace stems from inner peace.

We must cleanse ourselves of greed, hatred, and ignorance. These three poisons are the root behind all our sufferings.

The Teachings of Ven Master CHIN KUNG *in What is Buddhism?*

WHEN WE start on the Buddha's Path we begin to see our many faults and vices, not only the coarse ones but also the more subtle ones which may not have been so obvious. Before studying the Buddhist teachings, selfish motives when performing deeds of generosity were unnoticed. When the deep, underlying, impure motives for one's deeds are realised is that not a gain? A sudden change of character cannot be expected soon as a result of the Buddhist teachings, but what is unwholesome can be realised as unwholesome, and what is wholesome can be realised as wholesome. In that way there will be more truthfulness, more sincerity in our actions, speech and thoughts. The disadvantage and danger of unwholesomeness and the benefit of wholesomeness will be seen more and more clearly.

The Buddha's Path, Nina van Gorkom

WHEN A man considers this world as a bubble of froth, and as the illusion of an appearance, then the king of death has no power over him.
Come and look at this world. It is like a royal painted chariot wherein fools sink. The wise are not imprisoned in the chariot.

Dhammapada, 170, 171

IT IS easy to see the faults of others, but difficult to see one's own faults. One shows the faults of others like chaff winnowed in the wind, but one conceals one's own faults as a cunning gambler conceals his dice.

Dhammapada, 252

THE GREAT Way is not difficult
    for those who have no preferences.
When love and hate are both absent
    everything becomes clear and undistinguished.
Make the smallest distinction, however,
    and heaven and earth are set infinitely apart.
If you wish to see the truth
    then hold no opinions for or against anything.
To set up what you like against what you dislike
    is a disease of the mind.
When the deep meaning of things is not understood
    the mind's essential peace is disturbed to no avail.

Verses of the Faith Mind, CHIEN-CHIH SENG-TS'AN

WHAT MORE wonderful, glorious, miraculous, splendid thing can there be than this world? Every winter the trees go dormant – it is almost like death. Then spring comes, and everything comes back to life. Flowers bloom, leaves unfurl. Then summer arrives – it is glorious! After that fall comes with its vivid colours and tremendous beauty, then winter again, over and over. Every day the sun comes up, giving light for us to see and to make distinctions in colour and form. Then daylight fades and the darkness of night follows, making things almost indistinguishable until dawn comes again.

Of course, we can choose to feel that everything is awful. Every day is a bad day and we are always suffering. Why do we suffer? Nothing ever goes the way we want it to go: we want more or we want something else; we want ourselves to be different or others to be different. We are losing our bodies; they are growing old, decaying, falling apart, and everything looks grim, terrible. If we feel it is bad, everything becomes bad; if we feel it is good, then it all appears good.

The whole world is created from Mind. How we perceive it is the whole story …

The Eye Never Sleeps, DENNIS GENPO MERZEL

TRUSTING EXPERIENCE

EXPERIENCE AND AUTHORITY

I F A person has faith … he preserves truth when he says: 'My
faith is thus'; but he does not yet come to the definite
conclusion: 'Only this is true, everything else is false.' In this
way … we describe the preservation of truth. But as yet there is
no discovery of truth …

When (the student) has investigated (his teacher) and has
seen that he is purified from states based on delusion, then he
places faith in him; filled with faith he visits him and pays
respect to him; having paid respect to him, he gives ear; when
he gives ear, he hears the Dhamma (teaching); having heard the
Dhamma, he memorises it and examines the meaning of the
teachings he has memorised; when he examines their meaning,
he gains a reflective acceptance of those teachings; when he
has gained a reflective acceptance of those teachings, zeal
springs up; when zeal has sprung up, he applies his will; having
applied his will, he scrutinises; having scrutinised, he strives;
resolutely striving, he realises with the body the ultimate truth
and sees it by penetrating it with wisdom. In this way … there
is the discovery of truth.

Canki Sutta, 15, 20 (MN)

HOLD FAST to the truth as a lamp. Seek salvation alone in the truth. Look not for assistance to any one besides yourselves.

From the Buddha's Farewell Address

THE MORE you take what you've learned from books to look inside yourself, the less you'll see.

K. KHAO-SUAN-LUANG, *Looking Inward*

EMPTINESS HERE, Emptiness there,
but the infinite universe stands
always before our eyes.
Infinitely large and infinitely small;
no difference, for definitions have vanished
and no boundaries are seen
So too with Being and non-Being.
Don't waste time in doubts and arguments
that have nothing to do with this.

Verses on the Faith Mind, CHIEN-CHIH SENG-TS'AN

ONE OF the central tenets of Buddhism is that all created things are impermanent. Thus Buddhism, being a set of created teachings, is by its own definition impermanent ... Thus authenticity in Buddhism cannot be represented by a static tradition, taken over ready-made from others, and applied as a doctrine or dogma. Indeed, the Buddha's dying words referred to the necessity for each person to work on his or her own salvation. There is, in effect, no authenticity for the individual in Buddhism unless it has been verified in the light of personal experience.

DAVID FONTANA, *The Authority of Experience*

DO NOT think that the knowledge you presently possess is changeless, absolute truth. Avoid being narrow minded and bound to present views. Learn and practise non-attachment from views in order to be open to receive others' viewpoints. Truth is found in life and not merely in conceptual knowledge. Be ready to learn throughout your entire life and to observe reality in yourself and in the world at all times.

Peace is Every Step, THICH NHAT HANH

MAKING AN EFFORT?

MAKE YOUR thoughts into a plough,
    and make pleasure and pain into oxen.
Contemplate your body as the field,
    and contemplate the fruit, the bliss of the
Dharma-nature,
    coming forth night and day.
Make your concepts into a plough,
    your feelings of pleasure and pain into oxen.
Sow the seeds of the elements
    to ripen on the field of your body.
Exerting yourself on that field,
    work day and night!
The fruit, the bliss of the Dharma-nature
    will never end.

Buddha's Lions, ABHAYADATTA

IN BUDDHISM there is no place for using effort. Just be ordinary and nothing special. Eat your food, move your bowels, pass water, and when you're tired go and lie down. The ignorant will laugh at me, but the wise will understand.

LIN-CHI

THE *VINAYA* master You Yuan asked Zhao Zhou:
'Do you still practise spiritual cultivation?'
'I still practise.'
'How do you practise?'
'When rice comes, I eat; when tiredness comes, I sleep,' Zhao Zhou answered.
'Everyone does that; so everyone practises spiritual cultivation like you!'
'Not the same.'
'Why not the same?'
'When it's time to eat, they do not eat; they're tied down by hundreds of thoughts. When it's time to sleep, they do not sleep; they're troubled by thousands of calculating schemes.'

The Complete Book of Zen, WONG KIEW KIT

THE GREAT Way is calm and large-hearted,
For it nothing is easy, nothing hard;
Small views are irresolute, the more in haste, the tardier
they go.

CHIEN-CHIH SENG-TS'AN *'On believing in Mind'* in
Buddhist Scriptures, ed. CONZE

LET A wise man remove impurities from himself even as a
silversmith removes impurities from the silver: one by one,
little by little, again and again.

Dhammapada, 239

SUFFERING

HAVING BEEN born we get old and sick and then we die, and that's totally natural and normal … As soon as we're born, we're dead. Our birth and our death are just one thing. It's like a tree: when there's a root, there must be twigs. When there are twigs, there must be a root. You can't have one without the other. It's a little funny to see how at a death people are so grief-stricken and distracted, fearful and sad, and at a birth how happy and delighted. It's delusion; nobody has ever looked at this clearly. I think if you really want to cry, then it would be better to do so when someone is born. For actually birth is death, death is birth, the root is the twig, the twig is the root. If you've got to cry, cry at the root, cry at the birth.

AJAHN CHAH, *Entering the Stream*

BUDDHISM TEACHES that the road to liberation from the sufferings of birth and death lies in our awakening to the far broader life that lies beyond the confines of the finite self.

Unlocking the Mysteries of Birth and Death, DAISAKU IKEDA

WHEN TRAGEDY and misfortune come our way, as surely they must, it can be very helpful to make a comparison with another event, or to call to mind a similar or worse situation that has befallen, if not ourselves, then others before us. If we can actually shift our focus away from self and towards others, we experience a freeing effect. It seems there is something about the dynamics of self-absorption which tends to magnify the suffering of the one who is in that state. If we come to see our suffering in relation to that of others, we begin to recognise that, relatively speaking, it is not all that significant. This enables us to maintain our peace of mind much more easily than if we concentrate on our problems to the exclusion of all else.

Ancient Wisdom, Modern World, THE DALAI LAMA

I F THE prospect of confronting our suffering head-on can sometimes seem a bit daunting, it is very helpful to remember that nothing within the realm of what we commonly experience is permanent. All phenomena are subject to change and decay. Secondly, the interdependent nature of reality means that we are mistaken if we ever suppose that our experience of suffering – or happiness for that matter – can be attributed to a single source ... everything that is arises from innumerable causes and conditions.

Ancient Wisdom, Modern World, THE DALAI LAMA

FEELINGS

WHY BE unhappy about something
If it can be remedied?
And what is the use of being unhappy about
   something
If it cannot be remedied?

A Guide to the Bodhisattva's Way of Life, SHANTIDEVA

ONE NEED not have fears that one's focusing the mind on the feelings and emotions ... will lead to cold aloofness or an emotional withdrawal. On the contrary, mind and heart will become more open to all those finer emotions ... It will not exclude warm human relationships, nor the enjoyment of beauty in art and nature. But it will remove from them the fever of clinging, so that those experiences will give a deeper satisfaction, as far as the world of dukkha admits.

Contemplation of Feelings, NANAPONIKA *quoted in*
The Authority of Experience

WHEN WE reflect on our own desire and hatred, we see that they are generated within a conception of oneself as very solid, due to which there comes to be a strong distinction between oneself and others, and consequently attachment for one's own side and hatred of others. Attitudes of desire and hatred have an exaggerated thought of I as their basis, do they not?

The Meaning of Life from a Buddhist Perspective,
THE DALAI LAMA

THE MOST moving emotional experiences in therapy are those of the transference, in which it is revealed how earlier relationships are still shaping and defining present-day interactions, as demonstrated in the actual relationship with the therapist. The most moving experiences in meditation are those that enable the meditator to come face-to-face with various cherished images of self, only to reveal how ultimately lacking such images are.

Thoughts without a Thinker, MARK EPSTEIN

THE ABILITY to be both in and aside from the feeling, at the same time, is something that the Buddha taught his disciples to cultivate. He did not teach them to not have feelings. He taught them to allow the process to flow whilst also being able to observe it. The flow of feelings gives us essential information about our lives. To cut them off would be one extreme – the extreme of asceticism. To abandon ourselves to their control would be the other extreme – the extreme of indulgence. The Buddha taught a Middle Way between these two extremes, a middle current where life flows effectively. This teaching of observing feeling *while in the feelings* is given time and again in the Buddha's basic instructions on mindfulness.

The Feeling Buddha, DAVID BRAZIER

CULTIVATING THE MIND

THE MIND AND MEDITATION

EVEN AS rain breaks not through a well-thatched house, passions break not through a well-guarded mind.

Dhammapada, 13

JUST AS a lake fed by a spring, with no inflow from east, west, north or south, where the rain-god sends moderate showers from time to time, the water welling up from below, mingling with cool water, would suffuse, fill and irradiate that cool water, so that no part of the pool was untouched by it – so, with this delight and joy born of concentration he so suffuses his body that no spot remains untouched.

Samannaphala Sutta, 78 (DN)

BETTER THAN a hundred years lived in ignorance, without contemplation, is one single day of life lived in wisdom and in deep contemplation.

Dhammapada, 111

ALL ZEN students should devote themselves at the beginning to zazen (sitting meditation). Sitting in either the fully locked position or the half-locked position, with the eyes half-shut, see the original face which was before father or mother were born ... before heaven and earth were parted, before you received human form. What is called the original face will appear. The original face is without colour or form, like the empty sky in whose clarity there is no form ...

Every time a thought arises, throw it away. Just devote yourself to sweeping away the thoughts. Sweeping away thoughts means performing zazen. When thought is put down, the original face appears.

The Rinzai Zen Master, DAITO KOKUSH *in*
The Complete Book of Zen

AN ENEMY can hurt an enemy, and a man who hates can harm another man; but a man's own mind, if wrongly directed, can do him a far greater harm.

A father or a mother, or a relative, can indeed do good to a man; but his own right-directed mind can do to him a far greater good.

Dhammapada, 42, 43

NEVER SURRENDER to carelessness; never sink into weak pleasures and lust. Those who are watchful, in deep contemplation, reach in the end the joy supreme.

The wise man who by watchfulness conquers thoughtlessness is as one who free from sorrows ascends the palace of wisdom and there, from its high terrace, sees those in sorrow below; even as a wise strong man on the holy mountain might behold the many unwise far down below on the plain.

Dhammapada, 27, 28

HERE, QUITE secluded from sensual pleasures, secluded from unwholesome states, a Bhikkhu (monk) enters upon and abides in the first jhana (meditative state), which is accompanied by applied and sustained thought, with rapture born of seclusion. This is a rapture apart from sensual pleasures, apart from unwholesome states. Again, with the stilling of applied and sustained thought, a Bhikkhu enters upon and abides in the second jhana, which has self-confidence and singleness of mind without applied and sustained thought, with rapture and pleasure born of concentration. This too is a rapture apart from sensual pleasures, apart from unwholesome states.

Subha Sutta, 17 (MN)

JUST AS a skilled bath man or a bath man's apprentice heaps bath powder in a metal basin and, sprinkling it gradually with water, kneads it till the moisture wets his ball of bath powder, soaks it and pervades it inside and out, yet the ball itself does not ooze; so too a Bhikkhu (monk) makes the rapture and pleasure born of seclusion drench, steep, fill, and pervade this body, so that there is no part of his whole body unpervaded by the rapture and pleasure born of seclusion.

Mahasakuludayi Sutta, 25 (MN)

PEOPLE WHO are disturbed by sickness
Have no strength to do anything (useful),
Likewise those whose minds are disturbed by confusion
Have no strength to do anything (wholesome).
Whatever has been learnt, contemplated and meditated upon
By those whose minds lack alertness,
Just like water in a leaking vase,
Will not be retained in their memory.

A Guide to the Bodhisattva's Way of Life, SHANTIDEVA

EVEN THOSE who wish to find happiness and overcome
misery
Will wander with no aim nor meaning
If they do not comprehend the secret of the mind –
The paramount significance of Dharma.

This being so,
I shall hold and guard my mind well.
Without the discipline of guarding the mind,
What use are many other disciplines?

Just as I would be attentive and careful of a wound
When amidst a bustling uncontrolled crowd,
So I shall always guard the wound of my mind
When dwelling among harmful people.

A Guide to the Bodhisattva's Way of Life, SHANTIDEVA

WHAT IS the path to the company of Brahma (the divine realm)? Here ... a Bhikkhu (monk) abides pervading one quarter with a mind with loving-kindness, likewise the second, likewise the third, likewise the fourth; so above, below, around, and everywhere, and to all as to himself, he abides pervading the all-encompassing world with a mind imbued with loving-kindness, abundant, exalted, immeasurable, without hostility and without ill will.

Again ... a Bhikkhu abides pervading one quarter with a mind imbued with compassion ... with a mind imbued with appreciative joy ... with a mind imbued with equanimity ...

This is the path to the company of Brahma.

Dhananjani Sutta, 32–5 (MN)

UNRULY BEINGS are as (unlimited) as space:
They cannot possibly all be overcome,
But if I overcome thoughts of anger alone
This will be equivalent to vanquishing all foes.

Where would I possibly find enough leather
With which to cover the surface of the earth?
But (wearing) leather just on the soles of my shoes
Is equivalent to covering the earth with it.

Likewise it is not possible for me
To restrain the external course of things;
But should I restrain this mind of mine
What would be the need to restrain all else?

A Guide to the Bodhisattva's Way of Life, SHANTIDEVA

WHENEVER WE meet someone, or think of someone, we should remember the determination we made in the meditation session and cherish them sincerely. We should feel affectionate love for all living beings and always value their happiness and freedom. By training in this way many of the problems we experience in daily life will disappear, because most of our problems arise from regarding ourselves as more important than others.

A Meditation Handbook, GESHE KELSANG GYATSO

WHEN MINDFULNESS of breathing is developed and cultivated, it is of great fruit and benefit. When mindfulness of breathing is developed and cultivated, it fulfils the four foundations of mindfulness. When the four foundations of mindfulness are developed and cultivated, they fulfil the seven enlightenment factors. When the seven enlightenment factors are developed and cultivated, they fulfil true knowledge and deliverance.

Anapanasati Sutta, 15 (MN)

FOR AS long as possible one fixes the attention on the breath, without allowing any distractions to break the chain of awareness.

As meditators we find out at once how difficult this is. As soon as we try to keep the mind fixed on respiration, we begin to worry about the pain in the legs. As soon as we try to suppress all distracting thoughts, a thousand things jump into the mind: memories, plans, hopes, fears. One of these catches our attention, and after some time we realise that we have forgotten completely about breathing. We begin again with renewed determination, and again after a short time we realise that the mind has slipped away without our noticing.

Who is in control here? As soon as one begins this exercise it becomes very clear very quickly that in fact the mind is out of control. Like a spoiled child who reaches for one toy, becomes bored, and reaches for another, and then another, the mind keeps jumping from one thought, one object of attention to another, running away from reality.

This is the ingrained habit of the mind; this is what it has been doing all our lives. But once we start to investigate our true nature, the running away must stop.

S.N. GOENKA, *Entering the Stream*

HOW WELL has the Lord Buddha who knows and sees pointed out the four foundations of mindfulness for the attainment of that which is good! What are they? Here a monk abides contemplating the body as body, earnestly, clearly aware, mindful and having put away all hankering and fretting for the world. As he thus dwells contemplating his own body as body, he becomes perfectly concentrated and perfectly serene. Being thus calm and serene, he gains knowledge and vision externally of the bodies of others. He abides contemplating his own feelings as feelings ... he abides contemplating his own mind as mind ... he abides contemplating his own mind-objects as mind-objects, earnestly, clearly aware, mindful and having put away all hankering and fretting for the world ...

These are the four foundations of mindfulness well pointed out by the Lord Buddha who knows and sees, for the attainment of that which is good.

Janavasabha Sutta, 26 (DN)

WATCHING THE PRESENT MOMENT

LET NOT a person revive the past
Or on the future build his hopes,
For the past has been left behind
And the future has not been reached.
Instead with insight let him see
Each presently arisen state;
Let him know that and be sure of it,
Invincibly, unshakeably.
Today the effort must be made;
Tomorrow Death may come, who knows?
No bargain with Mortality
Can keep him and his hordes away,
But one who dwells thus ardently,
Relentlessly, by day, by night –
It is he, the Peaceful Sage has said,
Who has one fortunate attachment.

Bhaddekaratta Sutta, 3 (MN)

BUDDHA TOLD a parable in a sutra:
A man travelling across a field encountered a tiger. He fled, the tiger after him. Coming to a precipice, he caught hold of the root of a wild vine and swung himself down over the edge. The tiger sniffed at him from above. Trembling, the man looked down to where, far below, another tiger was waiting to eat him. Only the vine sustained him.

Two mice, one white and one black, little by little started to gnaw away at the vine. The man saw a luscious strawberry near him. Grasping the vine with one hand, he plucked the strawberry with the other. How sweet it tasted!

Zen Stories, 18

THE BREATH is a clear indicator of our inner life: a bridge between body and mind ... Learning to pay attention to the breath is the beginning of meditation. It is a means of noticing that we are alive, calming ourselves and returning to the here and now. Studying the breath makes us aware of our bodies and of their inter-dependence with the world. A little time devoted each day to conscious breathing ... will improve health and calm one's life.

Zen Therapy, DAVID BRAZIER

THE EVER-FLOWING stream of thoughts, feelings and intentions are an acquisition. The mind's essence though formless and empty, is nonetheless sensitive. It is the discovery of this sensitivity, known as Buddha-nature in many traditions, to which many meditative practices are directed. The goal being to go beyond forms and movements that have been impressed on the mind. It is thus a psychological project to disclose the capacity for non-discriminative awareness that forms the core of our mental life. This is hidden under layer upon layer of structures and processes that naturally gather to the sensitive core as we live and experience the complex and intrusive conditions of collective living.

The Authority of Experience, JOHN PICKERING

ENLIGHTENMENT, PEACE, and joy will not be granted by someone else. The well is within us, and if we dig deeply in the present moment, the water will spring forth. We must go back to the present moment in order to be really alive. When we practise conscious breathing, we practise going back to the present moment where everything is happening.

Peace is Every Step, THICH NHAT HANH

THE TRUTH keeps going along on its own. Sensations keep arising and then disbanding. If we focus right here – at the consciousness of the bare sensation of sights, sounds, smells, tastes and tactile sensations, we'll be able to gain insight quickly …

Eventually you have to come down to the awareness that everything simply arises, persists and then disbands. Make sure you stay focused on the disbanding. If you watch just the arising, you may get carried off on a tangent, but if you focus on the disbanding you'll see emptiness: Everything is disbanding every instant. No matter what you look at, no matter what you see, it's there for just an instant and then disbands. Then it arises again. Then it disbands. There's simply arising, knowing, disbanding.

When you keep looking, keep knowing like this at all times, you'll come to see that there are no big issues going on. There's just the issue of arising, persisting and disbanding. You don't have to label anything as good or bad. If you simply look in this way, it's no great weight on the heart. But if you go dragging in issues of good and bad, self and all that, then suffering starts in a big way.

Looking Inward, K. KHAO-SUAN-LUANG

IF WE are unaware of our present actions, we are condemned to repeating the mistakes of the past and can never succeed in attaining our dreams for the future. But if we can develop the ability to be aware of the present moment, we can use the past as a guide for ordering our actions in the future, so that we may attain our goal.

Dharma is the path of here-and-now. Therefore we must develop our ability to be aware of the present moment. The technique of *anapanasati* (mindfulness of breathing) is such a method. Practising it develops awareness of oneself in the here-and-now; at this moment breathing in, at this moment breathing out. By practising awareness of respiration, we become aware of the present moment.

S.N. GOENKA, *Entering the Stream*

WHILE WASHING the dishes one should only be washing the dishes, which means that while washing the dishes one should be completely aware of the fact that one is washing the dishes. At first glance, that might seem a little silly: why put so much stress on a simple thing? But that's the point. The fact that I am standing there washing these bowls is a wondrous reality. I'm being completely myself, following my breath, conscious of my presence, and conscious of my thoughts and actions.

The Miracle of Mindfulness, THICH NHAT HANH

DEVELOPING THE MIND

THOSE WITH limited views
are fearful and irresolute:
the faster they hurry, the slower they go.

Verses on the Faith Mind, CHIEN-CHIH SENG-TS'AN

YOU SHOULD not lose your self-sufficient state of mind. This does not mean a closed mind, but actually an empty mind and a ready mind. If your mind is empty, it is always ready for anything; it is open to everything. In the beginner's mind there are many possibilities; in the expert's mind there are few … This is also the real secret of the arts: always be a beginner. Be very very careful about this point. If you start to practise zazen, you will begin to appreciate your beginner's mind. It is the secret of Zen practice.

SHUNRYU SUZUKI, *'Zen Mind, Beginner's Mind'* in
Entering the Stream

BREATHE SLOWLY and deeply, following each breath, become one with the breath. Then let go of everything. Imagine yourself as a pebble which has been thrown into a river. The pebble sinks through the water effortlessly. Detached from everything, it falls by the shortest distance possible, finally reaching the bottom, the point of perfect rest. You are like the pebble which has let itself fall into the river, letting go of everything. At the centre of your being is your breath. You don't need to know the length of time it takes before reaching the point of complete rest on the bed of fine sand beneath the water. When you feel yourself resting like a pebble which has reached the riverbed, that is the point when you begin to find your own rest. You are no longer pushed or pulled by anything.

If you cannot find joy and peace in these very moments of sitting, then the future itself will only flow by as the river flows by, you will not be able to hold it back, you will be incapable of living the future when it has become the present. Joy and peace are the joy and peace possible in this very hour of sitting. If you cannot find it here, you won't find it anywhere. Don't chase after your thoughts as a shadow follows its object. Don't run after your thoughts. Find joy and peace in this very moment.

The Miracle of Mindfulness, THICH NHAT HANH

WHEN THE months of the rainy season come round, the rain-clouds soak this great earth with moisture, the rain goes on and on and the deity pours down water from above. Many thereupon regain their energies, the surface of this great earth is refreshed, thoroughly irrigated and soaked with moisture, and the water which is conveyed from above refreshes also the low-lying pieces of ground. In consequence this great earth, irrigated from above by the rain-clouds, in its turn irrigates the herbs, shrubs, plants and trees, with the result that many branches and leaves and much foliage sprout forth, and there are many flowers and fruits. This great earth emits a fragrant scent and becomes adorned with fountains, lakes and ponds which bear many flowers and fruits. Men and ghosts become contented when they enjoy those flowers and fruits and enjoy that scent. Just so, when a Bodhisattva comes face to face with this perfection of wisdom and makes efforts about it, then one should know that before long he will be irrigated by the cognition of the all-knowing, will clarify and reveal it, and he will moisten beings with his revelation of the supreme jewel of the Dharma.

The Questions of Suvikrantavikramin
(Shorter Prajnaparamita Texts)

THE OBJECTIVE of the Zen way of life is the experience of awakening or enlightenment ... in which man escapes from the paralysis, the double-bind, in which the dualistic idea of self-control and self-consciousness involves him. In this experience man overcomes his feeling of dividedness or separateness – not only from himself as the higher controlling self against the lower controlled self, but also from the total universe of other people and other things.

At this moment there is a sudden flash of psychological lightning. What should have been obvious all the time has leaped into full clarity, and the student runs to his master and, without the least difficulty, shows him his 'original face'. What happened? All the time the student had been paralysed by the ingrained conviction that he was one thing, and his mind, or thoughts, or sensations, another. Thus when faced with himself, he had always felt split in two – unable to show himself all of a piece, without contradiction. But now it has suddenly become a self-evident feeling that there is no separate thinker who 'has' or who controls the thoughts. Thinker and thoughts are the same.

'Zen and the Problem of Control' in *This Is It, ALAN WATTS*

STUDENTS WHO would like to study the way must not wish for easy practice. If you seek easy practice, you will for certain never reach the ground of truth or dig down to the place of treasure. Even teachers of old who had great capacity said that practice is difficult. You should know that the buddha way is vast and profound.

Moon in a Dewdrop, ZEN MASTER DOGEN

WESTERN BRAINS work, they work a great deal, but always in the direction of efficiency. In that way the mind puts itself at the service of the result. Like all servants, it renounces its independence. I'm talking about another form of spiritual life, more detached and deeper, free from the obsession of a goal to be reached. In a way, the universal invasion of technology, everywhere it goes, lessens the life of the mind.

The Power of Buddhism, THE DALAI LAMA

TEACHINGS

WORDS!
The Way is beyond language,
for in it there is
> no yesterday
> no tomorrow
> no today.

Verses on the Faith Mind, CHIEN-CHIH SENG-TS'AN

THE PURPOSE of Buddha's Teachings is to eradicate superstition and clear up people's misunderstandings about life.

The content in Shakyamuni Buddha's forty-nine years of teaching describes the true face of life and the universe. Life refers to oneself, universe refers to our living environment. The Teachings directly relate to our own lives and surroundings.

The Teachings of VEN MASTER CHIN KUNG *in*
What is Buddhism?

ONE BESTOWS the teachings
for the sake of the individual.

One prescribes the medicine
according to the illness.

VENERABLE TRIPITAKA MASTER HSUAN HUA

GIVEN THE fact that sentient beings are of such different dispositions and interests, there are indeed beings for whom the theory of a Creator God is suitable and helpful, and thus you should not make trouble for yourself worrying about working alongside such a person. A considerable number of people who believe in a Creator God have reached a state without selfishness, and this proves that different teachings bring beneficial results. When we look at the results, respect for different religions grows.

The Meaning of Life from a Buddhist Perspective,
THE DALAI LAMA

THEN THE Lord Buddha ... moved by compassion for beings, surveyed the world with his Buddha-eye. And he saw beings with little dust on their eyes and with much dust, with faculties sharp and dull, of good and bad dispositions, easy and hard to teach, and few of them living in fear of transgressions and of the next world. And just as in a pool of blue, red and white lotuses some are born in the water, grow in the water, and, not leaving the water, thrive in the water; some are born in the water and reach the surface; while some are born in the water and, having reached the surface, grow out of the water and are not polluted by it, in the same way, monks, the Lord Buddha Vipassi, surveying the world with his Budhha-eye, saw all beings with little on their eyes ...

Then, knowing his thought, the Great Brahma addressed the Lord Buddha Vipassi in these words:

> 'As on a mountain-peak a watcher sees the folk below,
> So, Man of Wisdom, seeing all, look down from Dhamma's heights!
> Free from woe, look on those who are sunk in grief, oppressed with birth and age.
> Arise, hero, victor in battle, leader of the caravan, traverse the world!
> Teach, O Lord, the Dhamma, and they will understand.'

Mahapadana Sutta, 3.5–7 (DN)

JUST AS the particles of precious metal
become well-fused by the smith,
so the various things you have studied
must melt together in your mind.

Buddha's Lions, ABHAYADATTA

STRIVING IS most helpful for the final arrival at truth …
Scrutiny is most helpful for striving …
Application of the will is most helpful for scrutiny …
Zeal is most helpful for application of will …
A reflective acceptance of the teachings is most
  helpful for zeal …
Examination of the meaning is most helpful for a
  reflective acceptance of the teachings …
Memorising of the teachings is most helpful for
  examining the meaning …
Hearing the Dhamma is most helpful for memorising
  the teachings …
Giving ear is most helpful for hearing the Dhamma …
Paying respect is most helpful for giving ear …
Visiting is most helpful for paying respect …
Faith is most helpful for visiting.

Canki Sutta, 22–33 (MN)

STUDY AND KNOWLEDGE

THOSE WHO possess a complete and proper understanding of life and the universe are called Buddhas or Bodhisattvas. Those who lack the understanding are called worldly people.

What is Buddhism?

TO STUDY the buddha way is to study the self.
To study the self is to forget the self.
To forget the self is to be enlightened by the ten
   thousand dharmas.
To be enlightened by the ten thousand dharmas
      is to free one's body and mind and those of
      others.
No trace of enlightenment remains, and this traceless
      enlightenment is continued forever.

Shobogenzo, ZEN MASTER DOGEN

TOO MUCH knowledge leads to overactivity;
Better to calm the mind.
The more you consider, the greater the loss;
Better to unify the mind.

Excessive thinking weakens the will.
The more you know, the more your mind is confused.
A confused mind gives rise to vexation.
The weakened will obstructs the Tao.

Merely reading books
Is of no lasting value.
Being inwardly proud
Brings the enmity of others.

Using speech
Or written words
To gain the praise of others
Is something most repulsive.

WANG MING

LIKE A physician who, though
skilful in prescribing medicine,
Is unable to cure his own illness …

Like one who counts the wealth of others,
But has not a penny of his own …

Like a person born in a King's palace,
Who still suffers hunger and cold …

Like a deaf musician playing tunes
Others enjoy but he himself does not hear …

Like a blind artist whose many drawings
Are displayed for others,
but he himself can never see …

Without practising the Dharma,
Much study is the same way.

Flower Adornment Sutra, Chapter 10

WHILE WE practise conscious breathing, our thinking will slow down, and we can give ourselves a real rest. Most of the time, we think too much, and mindful breathing helps us to be calm, relaxed and peaceful. It helps us stop thinking so much and stop being possessed by sorrows of the past and worries about the future. It enables us to be in touch with life, which is wonderful in the present moment.

Peace is Every Step, THICH NHAT HANH

GAINING WISDOM

SIMPLICITY AND HOLINESS

I F A man speaks many holy words but he speaks and does not, this thoughtless man cannot enjoy the life of holiness: he is like a cowherd who counts the cows of his master.

Whereas if a man speaks but a few holy words and yet he lives the life of those words, free from passion and hate and illusion – with right vision and a mind free, craving for nothing both now and hereafter – the life of this man is a life of holiness.

Dhammapada, 20

W HERFVER HOLY men dwell, that is indeed a place of joy – be it in the village, or in the forest, or in a valley or on the hills.

They make delightful the forests where other people could not dwell. Because they have not the burden of desires, they have that joy which others find not.

Dhammapada, 98, 99

I LIKE to walk alone on country paths, rice plants and wild grasses on both sides, putting each foot down on the earth in mindfulness, knowing that I walk on the wondrous earth. In such moments, existence is a miraculous and mysterious reality. People usually consider walking on water or in thin air a miracle. But I think the real miracle is not to walk either on water or in thin air, but to walk on earth. Every day we are engaged in a miracle which we don't even recognise: a blue sky, white clouds, green leaves, the black, curious eyes of a child – our own two eyes. All is a miracle.

The Miracle of Mindfulness, THICH NHAT HANH

HE WHO lives only for pleasures, and whose soul is not in harmony, who considers not the food he eats, is idle and has not the power of virtue – such a man is moved by Mara, is moved by selfish temptations, even as a weak tree is shaken by the wind.

But he who lives not for pleasures, and whose soul is in self-harmony, who eats and fasts with moderation, and has faith and the power of virtue – this man is not moved by temptations, as a great rock is not shaken by the wind.

Dhammapada, 7, 8

JUST AS a bird, wherever it goes, flies with its wings as its only burden, so too the Bhikkhu (monk) becomes content with robes to protect his body and with almsfood to maintain his stomach, and wherever he goes, he sets out taking only these with him.

Culahatthipadopama Sutta, 14 (MN)

RYOKAN, A Zen master, lived the simplest kind of life in a little hut at the foot of a mountain. One evening a thief visited the hut, only to discover there was nothing in it to steal.

Ryokan returned and caught him. 'You may have come a long way to visit me,' he told the prowler, 'and you should not go away empty handed. Please take my clothes as a gift.'

The thief was bewildered. He took the clothes and slunk away.

Ryokan sat naked, watching the moon. 'Poor fellow,' he mused, 'I wish I could give him this beautiful moon.'

Zen Stories, 9

I DO not say … that one is better because one is from an aristocratic family, nor do I say that one is worse because one is from an aristocratic family. I do not say that one is better because one is of great beauty, nor do I say that one is worse because one is of great beauty. I do not say that one is better because one is of great wealth, nor do I say that one is worse because one is of great wealth.

For … one of an aristocratic family may kill living beings, take what is not given, misconduct himself in sensual pleasures, speak falsely, speak maliciously, speak harshly, gossip, be covetous, have a mind of ill will, and hold wrong views. Therefore I do not say that one is better because one is from an aristocratic family. But also … one from an aristocratic family may abstain from killing living beings, from taking what is not given, from misconduct in sensual pleasures, from false speech, from malicious speech, from harsh speech, and from gossip, and he may be uncovetous, have a mind without ill will, and hold right views. Therefore I do not say that one is worse because one is from an aristocratic family.

Esukari Sutta, 8 (MN)

WATER BIRDS
going and coming
their traces disappear
but they never
forget their path.

Moon in a Dewdrop, ZEN MASTER DOGEN

WISDOM AND FOLLY

NAN-IN, a Japanese master during the Meiji era (1868–1912) received a university professor who came to inquire about Zen.

Nan-in served tea. He poured his visitor's cup full, and then kept on pouring.

The professor watched the overflow until he no longer could restrain himself. 'It is overfull. No more will go in!'

'Like the cup,' Nan-in said, 'you are full of your own opinions and speculations. How can I show you Zen unless you first empty your cup?'

Zen Stories, 1

WISDOM IS purified by morality, and morality is purified by wisdom: where one is, the other is, the moral man has wisdom and the wise man has morality, and the combination of morality and wisdom is called the highest thing in the world.

Sonadanda Sutta, (DN) 22

ALL MY life false and real, right and wrong tangled.
Playing with the moon, ridiculing wind, listening to
  birds ...
Many years wasted seeing the mountain covered with
  snow.
This winter I suddenly realise snow makes a
  mountain.

Moon in a Dewdrop, ZEN MASTER DOGEN

LITERATURE AND art
Are but busy gnats in the air;
Technique and ability
A solitary lamp in the sun.
Those able and talented ones
Are really stupid fellows.
Discarding the pure and simple
They drown in too much beauty.

WANG MING

IF ON the journey of life a man cannot find one who is better or at least as good as himself, let him joyfully travel alone: a fool cannot help him on his journey.

Dhammapada, 61

UNLESS REFUGE you take in the Buddha
    and find in Nirvana rest
Your life is but vanity – empty and desolate vanity.
To see the world is idle, and to enjoy life is empty.
The world, including mankind, is but like a phantom,
    and the hope of heaven is as a mirage.

Worldlings seek pleasures fattening themselves
    like caged fowl.
But the Buddhist sage flies up to the sun like the wild
    crane.
The fowl in the coop has food but will soon
    be boiled in the pot.
No provisions are given to the wild crane,
    but the heavens and the earth are his.

The Teachings of Buddha, PAUL CARUS

IF A fool can see his own folly, he in this at least is wise; but the fool who thinks he is wise, he indeed is the real fool.

If during the whole of his life a fool lives with a wise man, he never knows the path of wisdom as the spoon never knows the taste of the soup.

But if a man who watches and sees is only a moment with a wise man, he soon knows the path of wisdom, as the tongue knows the taste of the soup.

The fool who thinks he is wise goes through life with himself as the enemy, and he ever does wrong deeds which in the end bear bitter fruit.

Dhammapada, 63–66

IN SPRING wind
peach blossoms
begin to come apart.
Doubts do not grow
branches and leaves.

Moon in a Dewdrop, ZEN MASTER DOGEN

I SHOULD not give directions with one finger,
But instead indicate the way
Respectfully with my right arm
With all my fingers fully outstretched.

Nor should I wildly wave my arms about,
But should make my point
With slight gestures and a snap of fingers.
Otherwise I shall lose control.

A Guide to the Bodhisattva's Way of Life, SHANTIDEVA

WORSHIP

I TAKE my refuge in the Buddha,
and pray that with all beings I may
understand the Great Way, whereby the
Buddha-seed may forever thrive.

I take my refuge in the Dharma,
and pray that with all beings I may enter
deeply into the sutra-treasure, whereby
our wisdom may grow as vast as the ocean.

I take my refuge in the Sangha,
and pray that with all beings I may reign
in great multitudes and have nothing
to check the unimpeded progress of truth.

Avatamsaka Sutra

REVERENCING THE Buddha, we offer flowers:
Flowers that today are fresh and sweetly blooming,
Flowers that tomorrow are faded and fallen.
Our bodies too, like flowers, will pass away.

Traditional words when making an offering of flowers

OM
MANI
PADME
HUM

The mantra of Avalokiteshvara

PEACE AND SERENITY

FOR THE health of our body, we should keep it moving. In taking care of our mind, we should keep it at peace. Exercise and peace of mind are the key to living a fulfilling life.

The Teachings of VEN MASTER CHIN KUNG *in*
What is Buddhism?

ALTHOUGH WE walk all the time, our walking is usually more like running. When we walk like that, we print anxiety and sorrow on the Earth. We have to walk in a way that we only print peace and serenity on the Earth. We can all do this, provided that we want it very much. Any child can do it. If we can take one step like this, we can take two, three, four, and five. When we are able to take one step peacefully and happily, we are working for the cause of peace and happiness for the whole of humankind. Walking meditation is a wonderful practice.

Peace is Every Step, THICH NHAT HANH

WE CAN smile, breathe, walk, and eat our meals in a way that allows us to be in touch with the abundance of happiness that is available. We are very good at preparing to live, but not very good at living. We know how to sacrifice ten years for a diploma, and we are willing to work very hard to get a job, a car, a house, and so on. But we have difficulty remembering that we are alive in the present moment, the only moment there is for us to be alive. Every breath we take, every step we make, can be filled with peace, joy, and serenity. We need only to be awake, alive in the present moment.

Peace is Every Step, THICH NHAT HANH

RELIGION AND CULTURE

I T IS important to adopt the *essence* of Buddha's teaching, recognising that Buddhism as it is practised by Tibetans is influenced by Tibetan culture and thus it would be a mistake [for Westerners] to try to practise a Tibetanised form of Buddhism ... Instead of copying such cultural forms, you should remain within your own cultural forms and implement Buddha's teaching if you find something useful and effective in it. Keep working in your profession as a member of your community. Although the various centres that are already established are useful and should be maintained, it is not necessary for someone who wants to practise Buddhism even to join a particular centre.

The Meaning of Life from a Buddhist Perspective,
THE DALAI LAMA

W HEN CULTIVATING the pure mind, less time should be spent watching television and reading magazines.

The Teachings of VEN MASTER CHIN KUNG *in What is Buddhism?*

A UNIVERSITY student while visiting Gasan asked him: 'Have you ever read the Christian Bible?'

'No, read it to me,' said Gasan.

The student opened the Bible and read from St Matthew: 'And why take ye thought for raiment? Consider the lilies of the field, how they grow. They toil not, neither do they spin, and yet I say unto you that even Solomon in all his glory was not arrayed like one of these ... Take therefore no thought for the morrow, for the morrow shall take thought for the things of itself.'

Gasan said: 'Whoever uttered those words I consider an enlightened man.'

The student continued reading: 'Ask and it shall be given you, seek and ye shall find, knock and it shall be opened unto you. For everyone who asketh receiveth, and he that seeketh findeth, and to him that knocketh, it shall be opened.'

Gasan remarked: 'That is excellent. Whoever said that is not far from Buddhahood.'

Zen Stories, 16

I HAVE ACCUMULATED enough experience to be completely confident that the teachings of the Buddha are both relevant and useful to humanity. If a person puts them into practice, it is certain that not only they but others too will benefit. My meetings with many different sorts of people the world over have helped me realise that there are other faiths, and other cultures, no less capable than mine of enabling individuals to lead constructive and satisfying lives. What is more, I have come to the conclusion that whether or not a person is a religious believer does not matter much. Far more important is that they be a good human being.

Ancient Wisdom, Modern World, THE DALAI LAMA

GOING BEYOND
ILLUSIONS

ILLUSIONS

ALL WORLDLY things, when closely looked at,
Are but illusions seen in dreams.

The Surangama Sutra

IT IS not that life *is* an illusion; rather, it is *like* an illusion. Therefore, we can speak of many different types of discrepancy between the way things appear and the way they actually exist. For instance, something that is actually impermanent can appear to be permanent; also, sometimes things that are actually sources of pain appear to be sources of pleasure. These are types of conflict between the way things actually are and the way they appear. Also, in relation to the final reality, objects appear to exist inherently but actually lack such inherent existence; that is another level of discrepancy between appearance and fact.

The Meaning of Life from a Buddhist Perspective,
THE DALAI LAMA

OUR LIFE can be compared with the flux of a river. A river seems to keep its identity but in reality not one drop of water stays the same while the river is flowing on and on. In the same way what we call a 'person' seems to keep its identity, but in reality there are mere passing mental phenomena and physical phenomena. These phenomena arise because of their appropriate conditions and then fall away. It can be noticed that people have different characters, but what is called 'character' are phenomena which have been conditioned by phenomena in the past. Since our life is an unbroken series of moments of consciousness arising in succession, the past moments can condition the present moment and the present moment can condition the future moments. There were wholesome and unwholesome moments in the past and these condition the arising of wholesome and unwholesome moments today. What is learnt today is never lost, moments of understanding today can be accumulated and in that way understanding can develop.

The Buddha's Path, NINA VAN GORKOM

THE BUDDHA said: 'You are still using your clinging mind to listen to the Dharma; since, however, this Dharma is also causal, you fail to realise the Dharma-nature. This is like a man pointing a finger at the moon to show it to others who should follow the direction of the finger to look at the moon. If they look at the finger and mistake it for the moon, they lose (sight of) both the moon and the finger …'

The Surangama Sutra

ALTHOUGH TODAY I am healthy,
Well-nourished and unafflicted,
Life is momentary and deceptive:
The body is like an object on loan for but a minute.

A Guide to the Bodhisattva's Way of Life, SHANTIDEVA

INTERCONNECTEDNESS

ALL MISTAKES that are
And all the various kinds of evil
Arise through the force of conditions:
They do not govern themselves.

These conditions that assemble together
Have no intention to produce anything,
And neither does their product
Have the intention to be produced.

Hence everything is governed by other factors (which
      in turn) and governed by (others),
And in this way nothing governs itself.
Having understood this, I should not become angry
With phenomena that are like apparitions.

A Guide to the Bodhisattva's Way of Life, SHANTIDEVA

HUMANITY IS one single body, one living Buddha body. What touches one part of this body touches all. Touch one strand and the entire web vibrates. Humanity shares a single destiny. This sharing of destiny, this network of interdependence, is as infinite in scope as the reflections from the jewels of Indra's wondrous net. My life and yours are completely autonomous. Yet we each exist only in total resonance with all other beings.

The Ethics of Enlightenment, RONALD Y. NAKASONE

DUE TO the fundamental interconnectedness that lies at the heart of reality, your interest is also my interest. Thus my happiness is to a large extent dependent on yours. From this, it becomes clear that 'my' interests and 'your' interests are intimately connected. In a deep sense, they converge. Because of this, if we wish for our own happiness, we have to consider others. It is a practical necessity that we do so.

Ancient Wisdom, Modern World, THE DALAI LAMA

WHEN THIS is, that is
This arising, that arises
When this is not, that is not
This ceasing, that ceases.

Majjhima Nikaya

THE SIXTH Patriarch (Hui Neng) explains that since our mind when awakened is the undifferentiated cosmic reality which includes all sentient beings, we can save all of them by purifying our own mind. This is the Hua Yen doctrine of mutual interpenetration of simultaneously arising dharmas, where the whole universe can be contained in a mote of dust. This concept may seem outlandish, but modern physicists are even now seriously investigating it. The world renowned physicist David Bohm, for example, who proposes the explicate order where reality is separated as we normally experience it, and the implicate order where separateness vanishes and reality becomes an unbroken whole, says that 'everything interpenetrates everything'.

The Complete Book of Zen, WONG KIEW KIT

A MUTUALLY DEPENDENT universe means that each individual helps to sustain the world and shape its course of events. We are continually interacting with others and the world. The manner in which we think, speak, and behave issues karmic energy which acts upon the world. At the same time, we are moulded by events and nurtured by personalities we meet.

Mutuality and interdependence are the substance of our lives.

The Ethics of Enlightenment, RONALD Y. NAKASONE

NON-ATTACHMENT

To keep our mind pure and at peace is like keeping a pond clean and undisturbed. When the water is clear and still, it can reflect the sky, sun, and trees just as they are, without distortion. Our mind is the same. When we are polluted by greed, hatred, ignorance, and disturbed by discriminations and attachments, we distort our picture of reality and fail to see things as they are. Wrong perceptions of reality can prevent us from enjoying a clear and happy life.

Learn to turn the light around, reflect upon yourself and smooth your mind-pond still. Everything outside of ourselves are equal in themselves; the garbage does not feel it is unclean, and the flower does not know it is fragrant, there is no such thing as discrimination. We must let our mind be at peace without attachments, this is true happiness.

The Teachings of Ven Master Chin Kung *in*
What is Buddhism?

JUST AS a tree, though cut down, can grow again and again if its roots are undamaged and strong, in the same way if the roots of craving are not wholly uprooted sorrows will come again and again.

Wealth destroys the fool who seeks not the Beyond. Because of greed for wealth the fool destroys himself as if he were his own enemy.

Dhammapada, 338, 355

EVEN AS a great rock is not shaken by the wind, the wise man is not shaken by praise or by blame.

Even as a lake that is pure and peaceful and deep, so becomes the soul of the wise man when he hears the words of Dhamma (teaching).

Good men, at all times, surrender in truth all attachments. The holy spend not idle words on things of desire. When pleasures or pain come to them, the wise feel above pleasure and pain.

He who for himself and others craves not for sons or power or wealth, who puts not his own success before the success of righteousness, he is virtuous, and righteous, and wise.

Dhammapada, 81–85

TWO IDEAS are psychologically deep-rooted in man: self-protection and self-preservation. For self-protection man has created God, on whom he depends for his own protection, safety and security, just as a child depends on its parent. For self-preservation man has conceived the idea of an immortal Soul or *Atman*, which will last eternally. In his ignorance, weakness, fear, and desire, man needs these two things to console himself. Hence he clings to them deeply and fanatically.

What the Buddha Taught, WALPOLA RAHULA

A TREASURE that is laid up in a deep pit profits nothing and may easily be lost. The real treasure that is laid up through charity and piety, temperance, self-control, or deeds of merit, is hid secure and cannot pass away. It is never gained by wronging others, and no thief can steal it. At death the fleeting wealth of the world must be left, but this treasure of virtuous acts is taken with one. Let the wise do good deeds; they are a treasure that can never be lost.

The Teachings of Buddha, PAUL CARUS

IF FOR the sake of fame
I give away my wealth or get myself killed,
What can the mere words (of fame) do then:
Once I have died, to whom will they give pleasure?

When their sandcastles collapse,
Children howl in despair;
Likewise when my praise and reputation decline
My mind becomes like a little child.

Therefore the happiness that arises
From thinking, 'I am being praised,' is invalid.
It is only the behaviour of a child.

A Guide to the Bodhisattva's Way of Life, SHANTIDEVA

AMBITION AND competitiveness are a common cause of dissatisfaction. The ambitious schoolchild cannot rest content until he or she comes top of the class, nor the businessman until he has made his fortune. Clearly not everyone can come top; but for one person to win, others must lose. But even the winners are rarely satisfied for long; their ambition drives them on until they too are beaten, worn out or dead.

Another reason why we fail to satisfy all our desires is that they are often contradictory. For example, we may want both worldly success and a simple life, or fame and privacy, or rich food and a slim figure, or excitement and security. We may demand our own way all the time and still expect to be popular, or we may wish for Dharma realisations yet still covet a good reputation and material wealth.

Our desires often involve other people and this creates special complications. Many relationships break up because of unrealistic expectations and desires.

We seek perfection – the perfect society, the perfect home, the perfect partner – but perfection cannot be found in samsara (this world of change). Samsara promises much but can never deliver the satisfaction we long for. It is not possible for impure, transient objects to provide the lasting joy we seek. This can be attained only by thoroughly purifying our mind. Though ignorance is the fundamental cause, worldly desires are the fuel that perpetuates the fire of samsara; therefore it is essential to reduce our worldly desires by recognising their disadvantages.

A Meditation Handbook, GESHE KELSANG GYATSO

DEATH AND BEYOND

HIDDEN IN the mystery of consciousness, the mind, incorporeal, flies alone far away. Those who set their mind on harmony become free from the bonds of death.

Dhammapada, 37

IN OUR culture, we place a great emphasis on the continuance of life. But truly, death is not a fundamental milestone, only an incident, another wave. Vasubandhu, the great fifth century Indian patriarch, likened life to a wave. A wave, he writes, is created from the energy of the wind which passes over it. That wave which is created in turn produces the next wave. The energy, which is generated, does not end in a single creative burst, but continues endlessly influencing every other wave it meets.

In the same way that the energy of one wave generates another wave, the life force that created a particular human being will produce new life.

The Ethics of Enlightenment, RONALD Y. NAKASONE

WHEN RESPIRATION has completely stopped, one should firmly press the arteries of sleep and remind him with these words …

Oh child of noble family, listen. Now the pure luminosity of the dharmata is shining before you; recognise it. Oh child of noble family, at this moment your state of mind is by nature pure emptiness, it does not possess any nature whatever, neither substance nor quality such as colour, but it is pure emptiness; this is the dharmata, the female buddha Samantabhadri. But this state of mind is not just blank emptiness, it is unobstructed, sparkling, pure and vibrant; this mind is the male buddha Samantabhadra. These two, your mind whose nature is emptiness without any substance whatever, and your mind which is vibrant and luminous are inseparable; this is the dharmakaya of the buddha. This mind of yours is inseparable luminosity and emptiness in the form of a great mass of light, it has no birth or death, therefore it is the buddha of Immortal Light. To recognise this is all that is necessary. When you recognise this pure nature of your mind as the buddha, looking into your own mind is resting in the buddha-mind.

The Tibetan Book of the Dead

WHEN WE drop the fear of dying, we are no longer afraid to live, either, and we can live fully at last. And when it comes time to die, then that is just another part of living also. We can totally let go and die wholeheartedly. True living is letting go of body and mind every moment; allowing all things to exist just as they are; releasing everything, no longer being attached to any preferences.

The Eye Never Sleeps, DENNIS GENPO MERZEL

BASSUI WROTE the following letter to one of his disciples who was about to die:

'The essence of your mind is not born, so it will never die. It is not an existence, which is perishable. It is not an emptiness, which is a mere void. It has neither colour nor form. It enjoys no pleasures and suffers no pain.

'I know you are very ill. Like a good Zen student, you are facing that sickness squarely. You may not know exactly who is suffering, but question yourself: What is the essence of this mind? Think only of this. You will need no more. Covet nothing. Your end which is endless is as a snowflake dissolving into the pure air.'

Zen Stories, 95

'WHATEVER YOU may say … Reverend Kassapa, I still think there is no other world …'

'Have you any reason for this assertion, Prince?'

'I have, Reverend Kassapa.'

'What is that, Prince?'

'Reverend Kassapa, take the case that they bring a thief before me, a thief caught in the act, and say: "Here, Lord, is a thief caught in the act, sentence him to whatever punishment you wish." And I say: "Take this man and put him alive in a jar. Seal the mouth and close it with a damp skin, give it a thick covering of damp clay, put it in an oven and light the fire." And they do so. When we are sure the man is dead, we remove the jar, break the clay, uncover the mouth, and watch carefully: "Maybe we can see his soul escaping." But we do not see any soul escaping, and that is why, Reverend Kassapa, I believe there is no other world …'

'As to that, Prince, I will question you about it, and you shall reply as you think fit. Do you admit that when you have gone for your midday rest you have seen pleasant visions of parks, forests, delightful country and lotus-ponds?'

'I do, Reverend Kassapa.'

'And at that time are you not watched over by hunchbacks, dwarfs, young girls and maidens?'

'I am, Reverend Kassapa.'

'And do they observe your soul entering or leaving your body?'
'No, Reverend Kassapa.'
'So they do not see your soul entering or leaving your body even when you are alive. Therefore how could you see the soul of the dead man entering or leaving his body? Therefore, Prince, admit that there is another world ...'

Payasi Sutta, (DN) 14,15

WHEN THROUGH intense desire
I wander in samsara,
on the luminous light-path
of discriminating wisdom,
may Blessed Amitabha go before me,
his consort Pandaravasani behind me;
help me to cross the bardo's
dangerous pathway
and bring me to the perfect
buddha-state.

The Tibetan Book of the Dead

HERE, STUDENT, some man or woman is of an angry and irritable character; even when criticised a little, he is offended, becomes angry, hostile, and resentful, and displays anger, hate and bitterness. Because of performing and undertaking such action, on the dissolution of the body, after death, he reappears in a state of deprivation, in an unhappy destination, in perdition, in hell. But if instead he comes back to the human state, then wherever he is reborn he is ugly. This is the way, student, that leads to ugliness, namely one is of an angry and irritable character ...

But here, student, some man or woman is not of an angry and irritable character; even when criticised a little, he is not offended, does not become angry ... Because of performing such action ... he reappears in a happy destination, in the heavenly world. But if instead he comes back to the human state, then wherever he is reborn he is beautiful. This is the way, student, that leads to being beautiful, namely, one is not of an angry and irritable character ... does not display anger, hate and bitterness.

Culakammavibhanga Sutta, 9, 10 (MN)

AT THE Blessed Lord's final passing there was a great earthquake, terrible and hair-raising, accompanied by thunder. And Brahma Sahampati uttered this verse:

'All beings in the world, all bodies must break up:
Even the Teacher, peerless in the human world,
The mighty Lord and perfect Buddha's passed away.'

And Sakka, ruler of the devas, uttered this verse:

'Impermanent are compounded things, prone to rise and fall,
Having risen, they're destroyed, their passing truest bliss.'

And the Venerable Anuruddha uttered this verse:

'No breathing in and out – just with steadfast heart
The Sage who's free from lust has passed away to peace.
With mind unshaken he endured all pains:
By Nibbana the Illumined's mind is freed.'

And the Venerable Ananda uttered this verse:

'Terrible was the quaking, men's hair stood on end,
When the all-accomplished Buddha passed away.'

And those monks who had not yet overcome their passions wept and tore their hair, raising their arms, throwing themselves down and twisting and turning, crying: 'All too soon the Blessed Lord has passed away, all too soon the Well-Farer has passed away, all too soon the Eye of the World has disappeared!' But the monks who were free from craving

endured mindfully and clearly aware, saying: 'All compounded
things are impermanent – what is the use of this?'

Mahaparinibbana Sutta, 6.10 (DN)

H E IS happy in this world and he is happy in the next world:
the man who does good is happy in both worlds. He is glad,
and feels great gladness when he sees the good he has
done.

Dhammapada, 16

ALTHOUGH I may live happily for a long time
Through obtaining a great deal of material wealth,
I shall go forth empty-handed and destitute
Just like having been robbed by a thief.

A Guide to the Bodhisattva's Way of Life, SHANTIDEVA

YOU SHOULD know that owls, after repaying their former debts, are reborn as wayward men in the realm of human beings.

Inauspicious creatures ... are reborn as men with animal habits.

Foxes ... are reborn as vulgar men.

Venomous creatures ... are reborn as savages.

Tapeworms ... are reborn as vile men.

Creatures good for food ... are reborn as cowards.

Animals providing materials for wearing apparel ... are reborn as servile men.

Creatures through whom the future may be foretold ... are reborn as literary men.

Auspicious creatures ... are reborn as intelligent men.

Domestic animals ... are reborn as men versed in the ways of the world.

The Surangama Sutra

BEYOND OPINIONS

THE WAY is perfect like vast space
    where nothing is lacking and nothing is in
    excess.
Indeed, it is due to our choosing to accept or reject
    that we do not see the true nature of things.
Live neither in the entanglements of outer things,
    nor in the inner feeling of emptiness.
Be serene in the oneness of things
    and such erroneous views will disappear by
    themselves.
When you try to stop activity to achieve passivity
    your very effort fills you with activity.
As long as you remain in one extreme or the other,
    you will never know Oneness.

Those who do not live in the single Way
    fail in both activity and passivity,
    assertion and denial.
To deny the reality of things
    is to miss their reality.
The more you talk and think about it,
    the further astray you wander from the truth.

Stop talking and thinking
>   and there is nothing you will not be able to
>   know.
To return to the root is to find the meaning,
>   but to pursue appearances is to miss the source.
At the moment of inner enlightenment,
>   there is a going beyond appearance and
>   emptiness.
The changes that appear to occur in the empty world
>   we call real only because of our ignorance.
Do not search for the truth;
>   only cease to cherish opinions.

Verses on the Faith Mind, CHIEN-CHIH SENG-TS'AN

WHEREAS SOME ascetics and Brahmins remain addicted to disputation such as: 'You don't understand this doctrine and discipline – I do!' 'How could *you* understand this doctrine and discipline?' 'Your way is all wrong – mine is right!' 'I am consistent – you aren't!' 'You said last what you should have said first, and you said first what you should have said last!' 'What you took so long to think up has been refuted!' 'Your argument has been overthrown, you're defeated!'

'Go on, save your doctrine – get out of that if you can!' the ascetic Gotama refrains from such disputation.

Brahmajala Sutta, 1:18 (DN)

IF THE eye never sleeps,
    all dreams will naturally cease.
If the mind makes to discriminations,
    the ten thousand things
    are as they are, of single essence.
To understand the mystery of this One-essence
    is to be released from all entanglements.
When all things are seen equally
    the timeless Self-essence is reached.
No comparisons or analogies are possible
    in this causeless, relationless state.

Verses on the Faith Mind, CHIEN-CHIH SENG-TS'AN

ENLIGHTENMENT

'WHY DOES the enlightened man not stand on his feet and explain himself?'

'It is not necessary for speech to come from the tongue.'

The Gateless Gate, 20

ENLIGHTENMENT IS like the moon reflected on the water. The moon does not get wet, nor is the water broken. Although its light is wide and great, the moon is reflected even in a puddle an inch wide. The whole moon and the entire sky are reflected in dewdrops on the grass, or even in one drop of water. Enlightenment does not divide you, just as the moon does not break the water. You cannot hinder enlightenment, just as a drop of water does not hinder the moon in the sky.

The depth of the drop is the height of the moon. Each reflection, however long or short in duration, manifests the vastness of the dewdrop, and realises the limitlessness of the moonlight in the sky.

Moon in a Dewdrop, ZEN MASTER DOGEN

HEALTH IS the greatest possession. Contentment is the greatest treasure. Confidence is the greatest friend. Nirvana is the greatest joy.

Dhammapada, 204

WHAT, REVEREND sir, is that Nirvana like that can be illustrated by similes? Convince me with reasons according to which a thing that is can be illustrated by similes.'

'Is there, sire, what is called wind?'

'Yes, reverent sir.'

'Please, sire, show the wind by its colour or configuration or as thin or thick or long or short.'

'But it is not possible, reverend Nagasena, for the wind to be shown; for the wind cannot be grasped in the hand or touched; but yet there is the wind.'

'If, sire, it is not possible for the wind to be shown, well then, there is no wind.'

'I, reverend Nagasena, know that there is wind; I am convinced of it, but I am not able to show the wind.'

'Even so, sire, there is Nirvana; but it is not possible to show Nirvana by colour or configuration.'

From *The Questions of King Milinda* (*trans*. BURTT)

WE BECOME enlightened when we see through our blinding misperception. Through examination we see the once-rigid ego dissolve into fiction, and the solidity of our world turns fluid. In that lightness of the transparent self, we feel a new connectedness with the world. Freedom from enslavement to the ego as centre of the universe becomes the bliss of union with the free-flowing energy of the world. Beyond the tense pacts, conflicts and stand-offs between 'I' and 'you', 'they' or 'it,' there is a liberated 'we' flexibly interacting on the field of total freedom.

The word 'enlightenment' is a good equivalent for 'buddhahood' because it is both the intellectual accomplishment and the spiritual experience of complete awakening. Enlightenment is more than cognitive; it is emotional and moral, since the openness of wisdom brings happiness, which automatically releases the most positive emotions and generates benevolent actions.

Inner Revolution, ROBERT THURMAN

YOU ASK me what *nirvana* is. I would answer: *a certain quality of mind.*

THE DALAI LAMA

Enlightenment ❧ 215

WHETHER DIRECTLY or indirectly, I should not do
    anything
That is not for the benefit of others.
And solely for the sake of sentient beings
I should dedicate everything towards Awakening.

A Guide to the Bodhisattva's Way of Life, SHANTIDEVA

LIFE AT each moment encompasses both body and spirit and both self and environment of all sentient beings in every condition of life, as well as nonsentient beings – plants, sky and earth, on down to the most minute particles of dust. Life at each moment permeates the Universe and is revealed in all phenomena.

On Attaining Buddhahood, NICHIREN DAISHONIN

JUST AS a flash of lightning on a dark, cloudy night
For an instant brightly illuminates all,
Likewise in this world, through the might of Buddha,
A wholesome thought rarely and briefly appears.

From *A Guide to the Bodhisattva's Way of Life,* SHANTIDEVA

WHEN YOU gain any new insights, don't go getting excited. You can't let yourself get excited by them at all, because it doesn't take long for your insight to change – to change right now, before your very eyes. It's not going to change at some other time or place. It's changing right now. You have to know how to observe, how to acquaint yourself with the deceits of knowledge. Even when it's correct knowledge, you can't latch onto it.

Looking Inward, K. KHAO-SUAN-LUANG

SOURCES

A Buddhist's Manual, Ven Dr H. Saddhatissa, British Mahabodhi Society, 1976.

A Guide to the Bodhisattva's Way of Life (Bodhisattvachary-avatara) by Shantideva, translated by Stephen Batchelor, Library of Tibetan Works and Archives, 1979.

A Meditation Handbook, Geshe Kelsang Gyatso, Tharpa, 1990.

Ancient Wisdom, Modern World, The Dalai Lama, Little, Brown, 1999.

Awakening the Sleeping Buddha, The Twelfth Tai Situpa, Shambala, 1996.

Buddha's Lions, Abhayadatta (trans. J.B. Robinson) Dharma Publishing, 1979.

Buddhism: a brief introduction, based on the teachings of Venerable Tripitaka Master Hsuan Hua, Buddhist Text Translation Society, 1996.

Buddhist Scriptures, edited by Edward Conze, Penguin Books, 1959.

Catching a Feather on a Fan, John Crook, Element, 1991 (quotes are from 'Calming the Mind', by Wang Ming, 6th c CE).

Dhammapada, extracts are from the translation by Juan Mascaro, Penguin 1973.

Digha Nikaya, translation by Maurice Walshe, Wisdom Publications, 1987 (extracts are marked DN).

Entering the Stream, edited by Samuel Bercholz & Sherab Chodzin Kohn, Rider, 1994.

Heart of Wisdom, Geshe Kelsang Gyatso, Tharpa, 1986.

Inner Revolution, Robert Thurman, Rider, 1998.

Looking Inward, K. Khao-suan-luang, WAVE, 1995 (printed for free distribution).

Majjhima Nikaya (MN), extracts are from the translation by Bhikkhu Nanamoli & Bhikkhu Bodhi, Wisdom Publications, 1995.

Moon in a Dewdrop, Zen Master Dogen, Element Books, 1985.

Peace is Every Step, Thich Nhat Hanh, Rider, *1991.*

Pure Land Zen: the letters of Patriarch Yin Kuang, Amitabha Buddhist Society, Singapore, 1993.

The Authority of Experience, ed. John Pickering, Curzon, 1997.

The Buddha's Path, Nina van Gorkom, Triple Gem Press, 1994.

The Complete Book of Zen, Wong Kiew Kit, Element, 1998.

The Ethics of Enlightenment, Ronald Y. Nakasone, Dharma Cloud Publishers, 1990.

The Eye Never Sleeps, Dennis Genpo Merzel, Shambala, 1991 (includes the quotes from Chien-chih Seng Ts'an, the Third Patriarch).

The Feeling Buddha, David Brazier, Constable, 1997.

The Meaning of Life from a Buddhist Perspective, The Dalai Lama, Wisdom Publications, 1992.

The Miracle of Mindfulness, Thich Nhat Hanh, Rider, 1975.

The Power of Buddhism, The Dalai Lama, Newleaf, 1996.

The Short Prajnaparamita Texts, trans. Edward Conze, Luzac, 1973.

The Surangama Sutra (with commentary by Ch'an Master Han Shan), Brighthill Buddhist Center, Sri Lanka (for free distribution, no date given).

The Teachings of Buddha, compiled by Paul Carus, 1915; revised edition, Rider, 1998.

The Teachings of the Compassionate Buddha, E.A. Burtt, New American Library, 1955, (sources marked 'trans Burtt').

The Tibetan Book of the Dead, trans. Francesca Freemantle and Chogyan Trungpa, Shambala, 1992.

This Is It, Alan Watts, Rider, 1958.

Thoughts without a Thinker: psychotherapy from a Buddhist perspective, Mark Epstein, New York: Basic Books, date unknown.

Unlocking the Mysteries of Birth and Death, Daisaku Ikeda, Warner Books, 1988.

What is Buddhism? published by the Dallas Buddhist Association, 1994 (copyright free).

What the Buddha Taught, Walpola Rahula, Oneworld
   Publications, original edition 1959.
Zen Flesh, Zen Bones, compiled by Paul Reps, Penguin 1971
   (included *Zen Stories* and *The Gateless Gate*).
Zen Therapy, David Brazier, Constable, 1995.

ACKNOWLEDGEMENTS

The publisher would like to thank the following institutions for
assistance and permission to produce the following pictures:
Robert Harding Picture Library (pp. 29, 45, 61, 65, 85, 104,
121, 125, 152, 160, 180, 192, 216); The Hutchison Library (pp.
33, 97, 156, 208).

INDEX